THE GREAT DEPRESSION

THE GREAT DEPRESSION, 1929–1938: *Lessons for the 1980s*

Christian Saint-Etienne, 1951–

HOOVER INSTITUTION PRESS　　Stanford University Stanford, California

Hoover Press Publication 298

Copyright 1984 by the Board of Trustees of the
  Leland Stanford Junior University
First printing, 1984
Manufactured in the United States of America
88 87 86 85 84   9 8 7 6 5 4 3 2 1

Library of Congress Cataloging in Publication Data

Saint-Etienne, Christian, 1951–
  The Great Depression, 1929–1938.

  (Hoover Press publication)
  Bibliography: p.
  Includes index.
  1. Depressions—1929. 2. Economic history—1971–
I. Title.
HB3717 1929.S25 1984   338.5'42   84-4451
ISBN 0-8179-7981-6

Design by P. Kelley Baker

To Marc and Serge Saint-Etienne
       &
my late mother, Suzanne

Contents

List of Tables   ix
Preface   xiii
Acknowledgments   xvii
Abbreviations   xix

PART I.   THE GREAT DEPRESSION

1   The Evolution and Causes of the Great Depression   **3**

ECONOMIC CYCLES, 1919–1938   4
INTERNATIONAL FINANCIAL FLOWS AND
    EXCHANGE RATE POLICIES   21
INTERNATIONAL TRADE   26
EVENTS LEADING TO THE CRISIS
    IN THE UNITED STATES   29

2   Interwar Monetary and Fiscal Policies in the
    United States, France, and the United Kingdom   **34**

MONETARY POLICIES   34
FISCAL POLICIES AND REGULATORY PRACTICES   38

3   A Theoretical Appraisal of the Great Depression   **43**

STYLIZED FACTS AND IDENTIFIED CAUSES   46
THE COMPETING MODELS   50
THE MECHANISM OF THE DEPRESSION   55
CONCLUSIONS   57

PART II. THE GREAT STAGNATION

4   The Evolution and Causes of the Modern
Economic Crisis   **63**

    ECONOMIC CYCLES, 1960–1983   63
    INTERNATIONAL DEBT AND FINANCIAL FLOWS
      IN THE 1970S AND EARLY 1980S   72
    THE EVOLUTION OF INTERNATIONAL TRADE, 1960–1983   77
    THE U.S. GREAT RECESSION   79

5   Monetary, Fiscal, and Trade Policies of the
Industrial Countries   **84**

    ANALYTICAL FRAMEWORK   84
    ACTUAL POLICIES   87
    THE RISE IN PROTECTIONISM IN THE 1970S AND EARLY 1980S   91

6   Economic Forces and Institutions in the
1930s and 1980s   **94**

    THE MODERN STRUCTURAL CRISIS   95
    THE DISINFLATIONARY CRISIS OF 1980–1982   97
    IS A NEW GREAT DEPRESSION POSSIBLE?   99
    CONCLUSIONS   102

APPENDIXES

A   Alternative Scenarios for 1984–1986   **107**
B   Benefits of Free Trade   **111**
C   International Lending and the
International Financial System   **114**

    INTERNATIONAL COOPERATION OF LENDERS OF
      LAST RESORT AND OF BANK SUPERVISORS   114
    MULTILATERAL LENDING   116
    RULES FOR FURTHER INTERNATIONAL LENDING   117

    Notes   *119*
    Bibliography   *125*
    Index   *131*

Tables

1.1 UNITED STATES: BASIC STATISTICS, 1919–1939   5

1.2 UNITED KINGDOM: BASIC STATISTICS, 1920–1938   6

1.3 FRANCE: BASIC STATISTICS, 1920–1938   7

1.4 GERMANY: BASIC STATISTICS, 1929–1938   9

1.5 U.S. LABOR FORCE   10

1.6 U.S. GROSS DOMESTIC PRODUCT, 1919–1939   11

1.7 U.S. FARM INCOME AND AGRICULTURAL PRICES, 1914–1939   12

1.8 U.S. POPULATION BY REGIONS (RESIDENCE)   13

1.9 U.S. EXPORTS AND IMPORTS OF FARM PRODUCTS, 1919–1939   14

1.10 WORLD TRADE IN THE INTERWAR PERIOD   19

1.11 BRITISH CURRENT ACCOUNTS, 1920–1938   23

1.12 WORLD TRADE: VALUE, PRICE, AND QUANTUM, ANNUAL FIGURES, 1913–1938   27

1.13 WORLD TRADE: INDEXES OF VALUE, PRICE, AND QUANTUM BY PRINCIPAL GROUPS OF ARTICLES, 1929–1938   30–31

1.14 SHARE OF EXPORTS OF GOODS IN GNP, 1929–1938   32

2.1 U.S. GOVERNMENT FINANCES (ADMINISTRATIVE BUDGETS), 1919–1939   39

2.2 U.K. GOVERNMENT FINANCES (ADMINISTRATIVE BUDGETS), 1929–1939   40

2.3 FRENCH GOVERNMENT FINANCES (ADMINISTRATIVE BUDGETS), 1929–1939   41

3.1   NATIONAL INCOME AND PRODUCT ACCOUNTS OF THE
      UNITED STATES, 1929–1939   47

3.2   NATIONAL INCOME AND PRODUCT ACCOUNTS OF THE
      UNITED KINGDOM, 1929–1938   48

3.3   NATIONAL INCOME AND PRODUCT ACCOUNTS OF
      FRANCE, 1929–1938   49

3.4   SHARE OF EXPORTS OF GOODS IN GOODS-PRODUCING
      SECTOR, 1929–1938   50

3.5   COMPONENTS OF U.S. GROSS PRIVATE DOMESTIC
      INVESTMENT, 1929–1936   59

4.1   GDP IN CURRENT DOLLARS USING PPP, 1970–1981   65

4.2   SHARE IN OECD TOTALS: GDP IN CURRENT DOLLARS
      USING PPP, 1970–1981   65

4.3   SHARE OF THE COMPENSATION OF EMPLOYEES IN
      DOMESTIC FACTOR INCOMES   67

4.4   SHARES OF VALUE ADDED IN VARIOUS SECTORS
      IN GDP, 1960–1980   70

4.5   SHARE OF EMPLOYMENT IN VARIOUS SECTORS IN TOTAL
      CIVILIAN EMPLOYMENT OF OECD, 1960–1980   70

4.6   GROWTH IN REAL GNP IN SEVERAL GROUPS OF
      COUNTRIES, 1980–1984   70

4.7   GROWTH IN REAL GNP IN SEVERAL GROUPS OF DEVELOPING
      COUNTRIES, 1968–1983   73

4.8   CURRENT ACCOUNTS OF SEVERAL GROUPS OF
      COUNTRIES, 1973–1983   73

4.9   FINANCING OF CURRENT-ACCOUNT DEFICITS AND RESERVE
      ACCRETIONS OF THE NON-OIL
      DEVELOPING COUNTRIES, 1974–1983   74

4.10 SELECTED COMPONENTS OF BALANCES
      ON CURRENT ACCOUNTS OF THE NON-OIL
      DEVELOPING COUNTRIES, 1973–1983   74

4.11 NON-OIL DEVELOPING COUNTRIES: EXTERNAL
      DEBT, 1973–1983   76

4.12 SOURCES OF EXTERNAL FINANCING OF NON-OIL
      DEVELOPING COUNTRIES, 1978–1983   78

4.13 CLAIMS AND LIABILITIES OF BANKS IN THE
      BIS AREA WITH RESPECT TO NON-OIL
      DEVELOPING COUNTRIES, 1978–1982   78

4.14 SHARE OF EXPORTS OF GOODS AND SERVICES
IN GDP, 1960–1980   78

4.15 DIRECTION OF EXPORT FLOWS (GOODS), 1973–1981   80

4.16 EVOLUTION OF SOME U.S. AGGREGATES, 1971–1976   82

5.1 BALANCE SHEET OF THE BANKING SYSTEM   85

5.2 SEVEN INDUSTRIAL COUNTRIES: MONETARY
POLICIES, 1976–1982   87

5.3 GOVERNMENT SPENDING AS PERCENTAGE OF GDP, 1960–1980   89

5.4 CHANGES IN RELATIONSHIPS OF PUBLIC EXPENDITURE
TO NOMINAL GNP, 1965–1980   90

5.5 FISCAL DATA: SEVEN INDUSTRIAL COUNTRIES, 1978–1984   90

A.1 MEDIUM-TERM PROJECTIONS OF PAYMENTS BALANCES
ON CURRENT ACCOUNT: NON-OIL
DEVELOPING COUNTRIES, 1982–1986   109

A.2 MEDIUM-TERM PROJECTIONS OF DEBT BURDEN: NON-OIL
DEVELOPING COUNTRIES, 1982–1986   109

A.3 MEDIUM-TERM PROJECTIONS OF DEBT BURDEN WITH TRADE WAR:
NON-OIL DEVELOPING COUNTRIES, 1982–1986   110

Preface

The question of the relevance of the Great Depression to the modern period has been a recurrent one since the first and especially the second oil shock. The problem seems to reside less in avoiding a new depression, which appears unlikely, than in escaping global economic stagnation. This book will show that the Great Depression did not result from a combination of apocalyptic forces but from ineptitude and demagoguery or lack of courage in political decisionmaking. It will further show that although in the 1980s technical expertise has by and large replaced the ineptitude of the 1930s, the difficult questions faced in the modern period are not being properly addressed.

This book is divided into two independent parts. The Great Depression is studied in Part I (Chapters 1–3) and the modern economic crisis in Part II (Chapters 4–6). Justifying this sequential structure will give me the opportunity to contrast the main characteristics of the two periods. The first and foremost justification is that the causes and the consequences of the Great Depression can be identified with reasonable certainty, although the relative importance of the causes is still debated. We are, however, experiencing the consequences of the modern crisis. Therefore, we can describe the Great Depression but can only speculate about the modern crisis. Second, provided that the main characteristics of the modern crisis are kept in mind while reading the first part, the reader will be treated to the consequences of the causes of the Great Depression, acquiring in the process an intimate knowledge of how economic policy mistakes can lead several quarters or years later to catastrophic consequences. Let us now review the main characteristics of the two periods.

The United States dominated the world economy in the late 1920s, as it still does today. On average over 1925–1929, U.S. manufacturing production represented 42.5 percent of world manufacturing production; the second largest producer was Germany (11.5 percent), followed by the United Kingdom (9.5 percent) and France (6.6 percent). On average over 1980–1981, the U.S. share of the gross domestic product of the member-states of the Organization for Economic Cooperation and Development (OECD) was 38 percent, followed by Japan (14.5 percent), Germany (8.4 percent), and France (7.1 percent). Hence in the 1980s as in the 1930s, a depression must engulf the United States to be a world depression.

In 1929, the share of exports of goods alone in gross national product was 5 percent in the United States and about 14 percent in the United Kingdom, Germany, and France. In 1980, the share of exports of goods and services in gross domestic product was 10 percent in the United States and 17.5 percent for the seven largest industrial countries of the OECD (including the United States), reaching almost 30 percent for the European Economic Community. Hence, in the 1980s, even more than in the 1930s, the developed countries depend on a healthy world economy. Should an international trade war reduce world trade in the 1980s as it did in the 1930s, the consequences for the world would be devastating.

In the late 1920s, the states of Central and Eastern Europe were heavily indebted to American and British commercial banks. The prosperity of Germany in 1927–1929, for example, was remarkable; net investment was very large and averaged almost 12 percent of national income, but about half of the net investment was funded by foreign loans. When the German financial system collapsed in 1931, it brought down sterling and most of the world financial system with it. Still, in 1930 net foreign investments in Germany (only part of which was credit) represented 130 percent of German exports of goods alone. In 1983, the external debt of developing countries represented over 140 percent of their exports of goods and services—in the case of the Central and South Americas this ratio was a staggering 240 percent.

The collapse of the German financial system in June–July 1931 was the main cause forcing Great Britain to abandon the gold standard in September 1931; this explains the emphasis given in Chapter 1 to the economic crisis in Central Europe in the 1930s. However, with respect to the near-default of Mexico, Brazil, and other South American countries in 1982–1983, it should be kept in mind that in the 1930s, Mexico, Brazil, and other South American countries did default on their external debt obligations. Brazil declared a temporary moratorium on foreign debt payments on August 30, 1931, converting this later into a permanent default by issuing long-term bonds for the value of the unpaid interest obligations. On January 22, 1932, Mexico suspended all its debt-service obligations for three years. Peru (April 1931), Chile (July 1931), and almost all South and Central American countries partially or totally suspended foreign debt payments in 1931–1932. Settlements over the next fifteen years in South America were reached in some notable cases at about 10 percent of the original face value of the outstanding debts.

In an environment of economic interdependence dominated by the United States and marked by the fragile financial position of Central Europe, which needed to export to service its debt, and even though the United States had been enjoying a surplus in its international trade of goods and services of more than $1 billion (or about 1 percent of GNP) every year from 1927 to 1930, the president of the United States signed into law on June 17, 1930, one of the largest tariff increases in international trade history. In 1984, the U.S. deficit on international trade of goods and services is expected to be more than 2 percent of GNP and possibly larger than $80 billion. At the same time, the debt-servicing capacity of developing countries is so limited that while only fifteen countries rescheduled their commercial bank debt obligations in 1978–1981, there were seven such reschedulings in 1982 and twenty in the first ten months of 1983 alone.

The final item to keep in mind when the inability of the main countries to reach agreements to control the world economic situation in the 1930s is considered in Part I is the list of the international economic conferences that did not produce any long-lasting results from mid-1982 to mid-1983: the Versailles and Williamsburg summits, the General Agreement on Tariffs and Trade (GATT) ministerial negotiations in November 1982, and the Sixth Session of the United Nations Conference on Trade and Development (UNCTAD VI) in June–July 1983. The continuing triangular trade disputes between the United States, Japan, and Europe and the tensions over U.S. economic policies are a constant reminder of the fragility of international economic and financial arrangements.

Policy mistakes similar to those of the 1930s must be avoided, although their consequences would be somewhat different in the 1980s because of changed structures and institutions (see Chapter 6). Whether they will be avoided is one of the main questions and challenges of the 1980s.

The same analytical method is used throughout the book to ensure consistency of treatment of the Great Depression and the present economic crisis. First the essential, or "stylized," facts that need to be explained are established. Then the causes and mechanisms (or channels by which the causes lead to the consequences) are identified and discussed. Chapters 1 and 2 in Part I and Chapters 4 and 5 in Part II present a historical analysis of the facts, and Chapters 3 and 6 give an economic analysis of these facts. This book stresses the importance of decisionmaking under uncertainty and the role of the price system in allocating scarce resources in a world of uncertainty. Institutional factors are taken into account when necessary.

January 4, 1984

Acknowledgments

I wish to thank Andrew Crockett for extensive comments on the first draft (dated November 30, 1982) and on the second draft (dated February 15, 1983) of this manuscript, as well as Anna Schwartz and Edmond Alphandery for specific comments on the third draft (dated July 1, 1983). The fourth draft was fully updated as of January 3, 1984. I also wish to thank Richard Abrams, Barry Campbell, George von Furstenberg, Louis Goreux, Miranda Xafa, an anonymous IMF referee, and anonymous Hoover Institution referees for comments on part or all of the previous drafts. None of these readers can be held responsible for the contents of this volume. I wish to thank as well the Hoover Institution for publishing my work and for suggesting needed improvements.

Finally, I gratefully acknowledge the excellent typing of all the drafts by Carolyn Statham.

All views expressed are strictly those of the author and do not necessarily represent the opinions of other staff members or the executive directors of the International Monetary Fund.

Abbreviations

BIS	Bank for International Settlements
EEC	European Economic Community
GATT	General Agreement on Tariffs and Trade
GDP	Gross domestic product
GNP	Gross national product
IMF	International Monetary Fund
M1	Money stock: currency and demand deposits
M2	M1 and quasi-money stock (time deposits)
M3	M2 and long-term deposits and/or nonbank deposits (definition varies by country)
NBER	National Bureau of Economic Research
NIPA	National Income and Product Accounts
NIRA	National Industrial Recovery Act
OECD	Organization for Economic Cooperation and Development
OPEC	Organization of Petroleum Exporting Countries
PPP	Purchasing power parity
SDR	Special drawing right

Note: Throughout the text, "billion" is used in the American sense, that is, a thousand million.

PART I

THE GREAT DEPRESSION

1

The Evolution and Causes of the Great Depression

The decisionmakers of the 1930s had a very limited statistical base to help them understand the context and evolution of the Great Depression. For example, the National Income and Product Accounts (NIPA) and the money supply series of the United States, France, and Great Britain were constituted much later, for the most part in the 1960s and 1970s. What appear to informed economic analysts of the 1980s to be unbelievable policy mistakes were mostly the product of ignorance of the facts and partly the consequence of misguided interpretations of the available information. Since the basic statistics became available, a wealth of new works has appeared, and the beginning of a consensus on the causes of the Great Depression has emerged. But many differences remain.

I will try to show in what follows that a large part of the remaining differences could be bridged by taking proper account of two factors: the increase in uncertainty due to the collapse of the international economy and the institutional factors that allowed certain power groups to have a larger impact on decisionmaking than their relative weight should have permitted. I also attempt to trace the respective responsibilities of decisionmakers, whether from the government or the private sector, in starting and worsening the crisis.

Before 1913, European industries supplied the rest of the world with manufactures in exchange for raw materials and foodstuffs. In 1913, primary commodities represented between 80 and 85 percent of imports and manufactures between 60 and 70 percent of exports for the United Kingdom, Germany, and France.

During World War I, non-European countries increased their agricultural and industrial production to supply European markets as well as their own. The United States was the greatest beneficiary of this expansion; U.S.

imports from Europe remained below $900 million from 1913 to 1919 while U.S. exports to Europe increased from $1,500 million in 1913 to $5,200 million in 1919.

In the 1920s, following the postwar reconstruction of European industry, its reconversion to civilian output, and the return to full agricultural production, world markets for manufactures became very competitive, and oversupplies of foodstuffs depressed prices. Especially hurt were U.S. farmers.

This chapter reviews the economic cycles that marked the interwar economy, as well as the evolution of international financial flows and trade during the period and the sequence of events that led to the crisis. Attention focuses on the four main actors in the Great Depression: the United States, the United Kingdom, France, and Germany.

Economic Cycles, 1919–1938

The Evolution of Economic Activity in the 1920s

In early 1919, the world economy started to expand rapidly to replenish stocks and supply consumers, who had accumulated substantial savings during the war. Moreover, governments maintained a high level of expenditure, worsening the competition for scarce resources, and prices increased rapidly. Soon raw materials and foodstuffs began to arrive in Europe, and factories started to meet the pent-up demand. Worried about inflation, U.S. financial authorities took steps to restrict credit expansion, strongly increasing interest rates at the beginning of 1920. The growth of the quantity of M1 (currency and demand deposits), which slowed in the first half of 1920, turned negative after September. From 1920 to 1921, M1 fell by 9 percent in the United States. U.S. wholesale prices and industrial production contracted sharply, starting in the second half of 1920 and followed in 1921 in the United Kingdom and France (see Tables 1.1–1.3).

The U.S. economy began to recover in the second half of 1921. From the reference trough in July 1921 to the peak in May 1923, the Federal Reserve Board index of industrial production rose by 63 percent and the stock of money by 14 percent. During the next six years, until mid-1929, U.S. economic expansion was relatively steady, except for two mild recessions (May 1923–July 1924 and October 1926–November 1927). Contrary to popular belief, there was no such thing as the Roaring Twenties, at least in the United States and the United Kingdom. From 1925 to 1929, the quantity of money was kept stable in both countries (see Tables 1.1–1.2), by active policy in the United States and by the return in 1925 to the gold standard

TABLE I.I   UNITED STATES: BASIC STATISTICS, 1919–1939

	GDP[a]	IP[b]	r[c]	M1[d]	M2[e]	WP[f]	CP[g]
1919	71	66	5.37	82	67	145	101
1920	70	69	7.50	89	75	162	117
1921	69	52	6.62	81	71	102	104
1922	73	67	4.52	81	72	102	98
1923	82	79	5.07	86	79	106	100
1924	85	74	3.98	89	83	103	100
1925	87	83	4.02	96	90	109	102
1926	92	86	4.34	98	94	105	103
1927	93	86	4.11	98	96	100	101
1928	94	91	4.85	99	100	102	100
1929	100	100	5.85	100	100	100	100
1930	91	83	3.59	97	98	91	97
1931	86	69	2.64	91	92	77	89
1932	73	53	2.73	79	77	68	80
1933	71	64	1.73	75	69	69	76
1934	78	69	1.02	82	74	79	78
1935	88	79	0.75	97	84	84	80
1936	97	95	0.75	111	93	85	81
1937	105	103	0.94	116	98	91	84
1938	99	83	0.81	115	98	82	82
1939	107	100	0.59	128	106	81	81

SOURCES: U.S. Department of Commerce, *Historical Statistics of the United States, Colonial Times to 1970* (Washington, D.C.: Government Printing Office, 1975); and *Federal Reserve Bulletin*, December 1959.

[a]Real GDP (in constant prices), 1929 = 100. This series differs from the National Income and Product Accounts (NIPA), 1929–1976, published in 1981. But the NIPA began in 1929, and we need a consistent series over the interwar period. (See Table 3.1.)

[b]Industrial production index, 1929 = 100.

[c]Money market rate, prime commercial paper, four to six months.

[d]M1 = currency and demand deposits; annual averages, 1929 = 100.

[e]M2 = M1 and time deposits; annual averages, 1929 = 100.

[f]Wholesale prices, all commodities, 1929 = 100.

[g]Consumer prices, all items, 1929 = 100.

with an overvalued exchange rate in the United Kingdom; wholesale and consumer prices fluctuated mildly around a *downward* trend. Over the five-year period 1925–1929, the average annual rate of increase in the real gross domestic product (GDP) was 3 percent in the United States and 2 percent in Great Britain. This misperception of the economic activity probably stems from the frantic trading on the U.S. stock exchange in 1928 and early 1929.

TABLE 1.2   UNITED KINGDOM: BASIC STATISTICS, 1920–1938

	GDP[a]	IP[b]	r[c]	M1[d]	M2[d]	WP[e]	CP[f]
1920	87	100	5.42	108	98	224	142
1921	82	68	4.76	107	97	144	130
1922	85	81	2.30	100	93	116	111
1923	87	89	2.30	98	92	116	105
1924	90	91	2.95	97	92	121	104
1925	94	88	3.69	96	92	117	104
1926	90	78	4.25	97	94	108	104
1927	96	98	3.98	99	96	103	101
1928	98	94	3.86	102	100	102	101
1929	100	100	4.94	100	100	100	100
1930	100	92	2.49	103	105	88	96
1931	95	84	3.23	97	102	77	90
1932	95	84	1.84	108	113	75	88
1933	96	88	0.69	107	114	75	85
1934	103	99	0.81	109	118	77	86
1935	107	106	0.65	115	126	78	87
1936	110	116	0.69	123	135	83	90
1937	115	124	0.67	125	140	95	94
1938	118	116	0.68	123	141	89	95

SOURCES: C. H. Feinstein, *National Income, Expenditure and Output of the United Kingdom, 1885–1965* (Cambridge, Eng.: Cambridge University Press, 1972); Christian Saint-Etienne, *La France dans la grande crise, 1929–1939* (Ph.D. diss., Sorbonne, 1981); Susan Howson, *Domestic Monetary Management in Britain, 1919–1938* (Cambridge, Eng.: Cambridge University Press, 1975); and David Sheppard, *The Growth and Role of U.K. Financial Institutions* (London: Methuen & Co., 1971).
[a]Real GDP (in constant prices), 1929 = 100.
[b]Industrial production index, 1929 = 100.
[c]Average short rate (average three-month bill rate and rate on day-to-day money).
[d]Mix of end-of-period and annual averages, 1929 = 100.
[e]Wholesale prices, 1929 = 100.
[f]Consumer prices, 1929 = 100.

The case of France is different. In the belief that Germany would compensate for war damages by reparations, French authorities encouraged a speedy reconstruction through public loans. Government debt, which had grown considerably during the war, doubled between 1918 and 1923. When it became obvious that Germany could not pay reparations, it was perceived by the financial markets that the public debt could be repaid only through inflation: the franc plummeted until Raymond Poincaré was called to office on July 23, 1926, to redress the situation. As premier and finance minister, Poincaré enacted heavy tax increases and balanced the budget in 1926—the

TABLE 1.3   FRANCE: BASIC STATISTICS, 1920–1938

	GDP[a]	IP[b]	r[c]	M1[d]	M2[d]	WP[e]	CP[f]
1920	65	53	5.73	48	44	83	61
1921	64	49	5.79	47	43	57	55
1922	74	63	5.11	48	45	54	49
1923	78	69	5.00	51	48	69	54
1924	86	80	5.99	54	50	80	62
1925	87	80	6.53	70	64	90	70
1926	88	87	6.58	75	69	115	91
1927	87	83	5.22	85	80	101	91
1928	92	93	3.53	98	95	102	90
1929	100	100	3.50	100	100	100	100
1930	97	100	2.72	112	113	87	100
1931	93	88	2.11	118	125	74	100
1932	89	78	2.50	115	125	65	89
1933	93	85	2.50	108	120	62	85
1934	93	80	2.70	107	120	59	80
1935	90	78	3.40	100	115	56	72
1936	91	82	3.67	109	121	65	79
1937	96	86	3.81	118	129	90	100
1938	96	81	2.76	138	146	103	116

SOURCES: Jean-Jacques Carré, Paul Dubois, and Edmond Malinvaud, *La Croissance française* (Paris: Seuil, 1972); Alfred Sauvy, *Histoire économique de la France entre les deux guerres* (Paris: Fayard, 1965–1975); and Christian Saint-Etienne, *La France dans la grande crise, 1929–1939* (Ph.D. diss., Sorbonne, 1981).
[a]Real GDP (in constant prices), 1929 = 100.
[b]Industrial production index of Vincent in Sauvy, 1929 = 100.
[c]Discount rate, Central Bank.
[d]End-of-period stocks, 1929 = 100.
[e]Wholesale prices, 1929 = 100.
[f]Consumer prices, 1929 = 100.

first time since 1913. Poincaré realized that it was impossible to deflate the economy to return to the prewar parity. After the stabilization of 1927, the franc was officially devalued in June 1928 by 80 percent from the prewar parity, which had been maintained throughout the nineteenth century; Keynes hailed the decision as visionary. With the implicit write-off of debts and the return of confidence, the French economy boomed; from the second semester of 1927 to the first semester of 1930, French industrial production increased by 30 percent, and the French economy proved resilient to the Depression until 1931.

The genesis of the German hyperinflation of the early 1920s was the creation of money by the government to meet its expenses during and after the war. The exchange value of the mark fell rapidly due to an adverse balance of payments. Then budget and external deficits and indexation of money wages in 1922 and 1923 contributed to a destructive inflation. A new currency was introduced in November 1923, and the government drastically cut the budget deficit. An international loan in 1924, which marked the beginning of a phase of large capital inflows, helped stabilize the economy. At first, the return of confidence delayed the necessary adjustments—rising expectations of a return to normality made reform seem unnecessary. Reorganization of the heavy industries that had benefited the most from the rise in prices began in the second half of 1925 and continued in 1926. Germany had to wait until the middle of 1926 to start recovering from the monetary catastrophe. The prosperity of 1926–1928, which was largely financed by foreign borrowing, was remarkable: industrial production increased by 31 percent from the first semester of 1926 to the first semester of 1927 and stayed at this high level throughout most of 1928. Net investment was very large, averaging 11.8 percent of national income in 1927 and 1928; foreign loans funded about half of the net investment.

Overall, the period 1925–1929 appeared to contemporaries as a time of prosperity relative to the preceding decade—except to one politically powerful group, U.S. farmers.

The U.S. Farm Crisis

The U.S. farm sector did not suffer a crisis in absolute real terms in the 1920s, but it was affected by two relative crises: (1) after the exceptionally favorable terms of trade experienced during the war, there was a return to a more normal level of relative prices, comparable to that of the years preceding the war; (2) while the GDP of the farm sector increased only slightly through the 1920s, the GDP of the rest of the economy increased at a much faster trend rate of growth. Unfortunately, the farm sector was overrepresented in the U.S. Congress and was able to force political actions that played a sizable role in starting and prolonging the Great Depression.

The U.S. farm sector did not suffer a crisis in employment and output in absolute real terms in the 1920s. The labor force employed in the farm sector was almost perfectly stable at 10.5 million from 1919 to 1929 (see Table 1.5), and real GDP (in constant-dollar prices) increased slightly from 1919–1920 to 1927–1929 (see Table 1.6). On the other hand, the terms of trade, which had been exceptionally favorable during World War I due to international shortages, returned to normal levels in the 1920s. The ratio of prices received for all farm products to prices paid (including interest, taxes, and

TABLE 1.4   GERMANY: BASIC STATISTICS, 1929–1938

	IP^a	r^b	$M1^c$	$M2^c$	WP^d	CP^e
1929	100	6.87	100	100	100	100
1930	86	4.43	97	93	91	96
1931	68	6.14	94	76	81	88
1932	53	4.95	83	70	70	78
1933	61	3.88	81	68	68	77
1934	80	3.77	89	73	72	79
1935	94	3.15	91	74	74	80
1936	106	2.96	97	78	76	81
1937	117	2.91	104	84	77	81
1938	126	2.81	n.a.	n.a.	77	82

SOURCE: Christian Saint-Etienne, *La France dans la grande crise, 1929–1939* (Ph.D. diss., Sorbonne, 1981); author's calculations based on League of Nations data.
NOTE: Data for pre-1929 period are too fragmentary to allow completion of series.
[a]Industrial production index, 1929 = 100.
[b]Private discount rate, 56–90-day bills.
[c]End-of-period stocks, 1929 = 100.
[d]Wholesale prices, 1929 = 100.
[e]Consumer prices, 1929 = 100.

wage rates), which stood on average at 107 (1929 = 100) from 1910 to 1915, increased to an average of 124 from 1916 to 1919 before falling to 98.5 from 1920 to 1929 (with a very small deviation around the average from 1922 to 1929; see Table 1.7). Although the overall terms of trade were not too unfavorable for the farm sector in the 1920s, some commodities traded on the international market faced renewed competition. International competition for such commodities as wheat and cotton was stiffer due to increased productivity and enlarged acreage. The wholesale price of wheat, which had reached 198 on average (1929 = 100) in 1917–1920, fell to 103 in 1921–1924 before increasing to 141 in 1925; it then fell regularly to 100 in 1929. The wholesale price of cotton, which stood at 159 on average (1929 = 100) in 1917–1920 and 152 in 1923–1924, fell to 102 in 1925–1929 (see Table 1.7). It is clear that the terms of trade were unfavorable in the second half of the 1920s for wheat growers, who politically dominated the rural population of the North Central region of the United States, and for cotton growers, who politically dominated the rural population of the South (see Table 1.8).

Another factor played an essential role in what U.S. farmers perceived as a farm crisis. While the growth of the real GDP of the farm sector was only

TABLE 1.5   U.S. LABOR FORCE

(IN THOUSANDS OF PERSONS, 14 YEARS OLD
AND OVER; ANNUAL AVERAGES)

	Civilian labor force (CLF)	EMPLOYED		UNEMPLOYED	
		Total	Agricul-tural	Total	Percentage of CLF
1914	39,401	36,281	10,945	3,120	7.9
1919	39,696	39,150	10,498	546	1.4
1920	41,340	39,208	10,440	2,132	5.2
1921	41,979	37,061	10,443	4,918	11.7
1922	42,496	39,637	10,561	2,859	6.7
1923	43,444	42,395	10,621	1,049	2.4
1924	44,235	42,045	10,599	2,190	5.0
1925	45,169	43,716	10,662	1,453	3.2
1926	45,629	44,828	10,690	801	1.8
1927	46,375	44,856	10,529	1,519	3.3
1928	47,105	45,123	10,497	1,982	4.2
1929	47,757	46,207	10,541	1,550	3.2
1930	48,523	44,183	10,340	4,340	8.9
1931	49,325	41,305	10,240	8,020	16.3
1932	50,098	38,038	10,120	12,060	24.1
1933	50,882	38,052	10,090	12,830	25.2
1934	51,650	40,310	9,990	11,340	22.0
1935	52,283	41,673	10,110	10,610	20.3
1936	53,019	43,989	10,090	9,030	17.0
1937	53,768	46,068	10,000	7,700	14.3
1938	54,532	44,142	9,840	10,390	19.1
1939	55,218	45,738	9,710	9,480	17.2

SOURCE: U.S. Department of Commerce, *Historical Statistics of the United States, Colonial Times to 1970* (Washington, D.C.: Government Printing Office, 1975).

about 1 percent on average from 1920 to 1929, the U.S. real GDP was increasing at an average annual rate of about 4 percent over the same period (see Table 1.1). This relatively poor performance exacerbated the differences between a more liberal urban population and a more conservative rural population.

Thanks to their overrepresentation in the U.S. Congress, farmers were able to press for much stronger action than would have been warranted by a rational analysis of the situation. Even though the United States was urbanizing rapidly between 1910 and 1930 (see Table 1.8), no reapportionment of representatives to the U.S. Congress was made after the census of 1920. The last reapportionment dated from an act of August 8, 1911, based on the

TABLE 1.6   U.S. GROSS DOMESTIC PRODUCT, 1919–1939
(IN BILLIONS OF DOLLARS, 1929 PRICES)

	Total	Farm sector	Percentage of farm sector in total
1919	73.6	9.7	13.2
1920	72.9	9.5	13.0
1921	71.3	9.0	12.6
1922	75.2	9.6	12.8
1923	85.1	10.2	12.0
1924	87.7	9.7	11.1
1925	89.8	10.4	11.6
1926	95.7	10.3	10.8
1927	96.6	10.6	11.0
1928	97.7	10.4	10.6
1929	103.6	10.7	10.3
1930	94.4	10.0	10.6
1931	88.8	11.2	12.6
1932	75.9	10.7	14.1
1933	73.8	11.0	14.9
1934	80.4	9.5	11.8
1935	91.0	10.4	11.4
1936	100.5	9.8	9.8
1937	108.8	10.9	10.0
1938	102.8	11.4	11.1
1939	110.6	11.5	10.4

SOURCE: See Table 1.5.

census of 1910. As a consequence of historically major significance, the apportionment of representatives in the 71st U.S. Congress (April 1929 to March 1931) was based on a population count that greatly advantaged the rural populations of the North Central region and the South. The Senate traditionally supported farm interests. This institutional reality made the concerns of the farmers the overriding political objective of the Congress.

In 1930, farmers were frustrated and politically powerful; they also thought they had a way to solve their problems. Farm exports as a percentage of farm income fell from 27.2 percent in 1919–1921 to 20.3 percent in 1922–1925 to 16.7 percent in 1926–1929. The balance of trade of farm products, which was positive until 1922, turned negative for the rest of the 1920s except in 1925 (see Table 1.9). The deficit increased to $400 million in the fiscal year ending June 30, 1930. Increased tariffs were the solution found by the farm lobby. During the presidential election campaign of 1928,

TABLE 1.7   U.S. FARM INCOME AND AGRICULTURAL PRICES, 1914–1939

	REALIZED NET INCOME OF FARM OPERATORS FROM FARMING (IN MILLIONS OF DOLLARS)	INDEXES OF PRICES RECEIVED AND PAID BY FARMERS, 1929 = 100			WHOLESALE PRICES OF SELECTED COMMODITIES (IN DOLLARS PER UNIT)	
		Prices paid, including interest, taxes, and wage rates	Prices received, all farm products	Ratio of prices received to prices paid	Wheat (bu)	Raw cotton (lb)
1914	3,764	64	69	1.08	0.939	0.121
1915	3,980	66	67	1.02	1.290	0.102
1916	4,908	72	81	1.13	1.329	0.145
1917	7,318	91	121	1.33	2.296	0.235
1918	9,040	108	140	1.30	2.159	0.318
1919	9,587	123	147	1.20	2.418	0.325
1920	7,107	134	143	1.07	2.455	0.339
1921	3,935	96	84	0.88	1.326	0.151
1922	4,445	94	90	0.96	1.213	0.212
1923	5,113	98	97	0.99	1.112	0.293
1924	5,338	100	97	0.97	1.232	0.287
1925	6,369	102	105	1.03	1.670	0.235
1926	5,930	100	98	0.98	1.496	0.175
1927	5,874	98	95	0.97	1.372	0.176
1928	5,841	100	100	1.00	1.324	0.200
1929	6,274	100	100	1.00	1.180	0.191
1930	4,528	94	84	0.89	0.900	0.135
1931	2,884	81	59	0.73	0.606	0.085
1932	1,922	70	45	0.64	0.494	0.064
1933	2,749	68	48	0.71	0.724	0.087
1934	3,853	74	60	0.81	0.932	0.123
1935	4,580	77	74	0.96	1.040	0.119
1936	5,114	77	78	1.01	1.123	0.121
1937	5,189	81	83	1.02	1.201	0.114
1938	4,229	77	66	0.86	0.777	0.087
1939	4,319	77	64	0.83	0.755	0.095

SOURCE: See Table 1.5.

TABLE 1.8   U.S. POPULATION BY REGIONS (RESIDENCE[a])
(IN THOUSANDS)

	Total	Urban	Rural	Percentage rural
Northeast[b]				
1910	25,868	18,563	7,305	28.2
1920	29,662	22,404	7,258	24.5
1930	34,427	26,707	7,720	22.4
North Central[c]				
1910	29,888	13,487	16,401	54.9
1920	34,020	17,776	16,244	47.7
1930	38,594	22,351	16,243	42.1
South				
1910	29,390	6,623	22,767	77.5
1920	33,126	9,300	23,826	71.9
1930	37,857	12,904	24,953	65.9
West[d]				
1910	7,082	3,391	3,691	52.1
1920	9,213	4,773	4,440	48.2
1930	12,324	7,199	5,125	41.6
Total U.S.				
1910	92,228	42,064	50,164	54.4
1920	106,021	54,253	51,768	48.8
1930	123,202	69,161	54,041	43.9

SOURCE: See Table 1.5.

[a]In censuses prior to 1950, the urban population comprised all persons living in incorporated places of 2,500 or more and areas classified as urban under special rules relating to population size and density.

[b]Northeast: New England, New York, New Jersey, and Pennsylvania.

[c]North Central: Ohio, Indiana, Illinois, Michigan, Wisconsin, Minnesota, Iowa, Missouri, North Dakota, South Dakota, Nebraska, and Kansas.

[d]West: Montana, Idaho, Wyoming, Colorado, New Mexico, Arizona, Utah, Nevada, Washington, Oregon, California, Alaska, and Hawaii.

Herbert Hoover acknowledged the claims of farmers and promised to enact a farm-relief program and an upward revision of the existing tariff. Hoover and the Republicans won a landslide victory and in mid-1929 enacted the Agricultural Marketing Act in an attempt to stabilize farm prices, but the question of the tariff remained in dispute. After a year of debate, Congress passed the Hawley-Smoot Tariff, which was much stiffer than Hoover wanted. The duties on agricultural products, including sugar, wheat, long-staple cotton, meat, and dairy products, were generally increased. Although

TABLE 1.9   U.S. EXPORTS AND IMPORTS OF FARM PRODUCTS, 1919–1939
(IN MILLIONS OF DOLLARS, ROUNDED TO NEAREST
TEN MILLION, FOR YEARS ENDING JUNE 30)

	EXPORTS		IMPORTS FOR CONSUMPTION	
	Value	Percentage of all exports	Value	Percentage of all imports
1919	3,580	51	1,930	62
1920	3,850	48	3,410	65
1921	2,610	41	2,060	56
1922	1,920	52	1,370	53
1923	1,800	46	2,080	55
1924	1,870	44	1,880	53
1925	2,280	48	2,060	54
1926	1,890	41	2,530	57
1927	1,910	39	2,280	54
1928	1,820	38	2,190	53
1929	1,850	35	2,180	51
1930	1,500	32	1,900	49
1931	1,040	34	1,160	48
1932	750	39	830	48
1933	590	42	610	52
1934	790	39	840	50
1935	670	32	930	52
1936	770	32	1,140	52
1937	730	26	1,540	53
1938	890	27	1,160	50
1939	680	24	1,000	48

SOURCE: See Table 1.5.

the majority of rates on manufactured goods were left unchanged, there were important increases in some goods, such as cotton, wool, and silk goods. Hoover received protests from 33 foreign governments, a great number of industries with foreign markets, and over a thousand economists throughout the United States. But he signed the bill on June 17, 1930, a congressional election year, disregarding the devastatingly correct forecast of the thousand economists, who had written in the *New York Times* of May 5, 1930:

 There are already many evidences that such action would inevitably provoke other countries to pay us back in kind by levying retaliatory duties against our goods. There are few more ironical spectacles than that of the

American Government as it seeks, on the one hand, to promote exports through the activity of the Bureau of Foreign and Domestic Commerce, while, on the other hand, by increasing tariffs it makes exportation even more difficult.

We do not believe that American manufacturers, in general, need higher tariffs. Already our factories supply our people with over 96 percent of the manufactured goods which they consume, and our own producers look to foreign markets to absorb the increasing output of their machines.

Further barriers to trade will serve them not well, but ill . . . America is now facing the problem of unemployment. The proponents of higher tariffs claim that an increase in rates will give work to the idle. This is not true. We cannot increase employment by restrictive trade.

. . . Finally, we would urge our government to consider the bitterness which a policy of higher tariffs would inevitably inject into our international relations . . . A tariff wall does not furnish good soil for the growth of world peace.

The ratio of duties to dutiable imports, which stood on average at 38.9 percent in 1925–1929, jumped to 44.7 percent in 1930, 53.2 percent in 1931, and 59.1 percent in 1932—a 52 percent increase over the average level in the second half of the 1920s. According to Sidney Ratner, an American economist and historian:

Much to the surprise of the American public, the Hawley-Smoot Tariff Act produced a world-wide tariff retaliatory movement against the United States. As a consequence of World War I the United States had become the world's greatest creditor nation and had maintained its large export trade through extensive loans to and investments in industrial and nonindustrial countries. This policy had permitted European countries to maintain their unfavorable trade balances with the United States and to continue war debt payments until the Great Depression of 1929. But when the United States ceased making foreign loans in the late 1920s and put through its upward revision of the tariff in 1930, the result was to cut down the imports from abroad, to increase even more the deficient trade balance of Europe with the United States, and to make more difficult the transfer of money payments to the United States. Hence, many countries resorted to "defensive" tariffs in order to create export balances for debt payment, to check domestic price declines, and to stabilize their national economies.[1]

The impact on the U.S. farm sector was immediate. Farm exports as a percentage of farm income stood at 16.7 percent in 1926–1929 but fell to 11.2 percent in 1930–1939. The balance of trade of farm products, which had been negative in the late 1920s, remained negative throughout the 1930s (see Table 1.9), and exports of agricultural commodities fell by 68 percent from 1929 to 1933. The crisis, which was brought about in large part by the tariff war, hit U.S. industry hard. But U.S. farmers did not benefit from this either: the ratio of prices received for all farm products to the prices paid (including interest, taxes, and wage rates), which had been remarkably stable at 98.5 (1929 = 100) in 1920–1929, fell to 74.3, or by a quarter, on average, in 1930–1933. The Republicans, who had served the farm lobby so well, lost control of the House of Representatives in the elections of 1930 and suffered a landslide defeat at the hands of the Democrats in 1932.

The Economic Problems of Central Europe

Like the U.S. farm sector, Central European economies were experiencing difficulties in the late 1920s. The dissolution of the Austro-Hungarian empire after World War I gave birth to countries whose national economies were not viable. Austria collapsed first, and Hungary followed it in hyperinflation. Both countries' finances were put under international control until restoration of external equilibrium was achieved in 1925–1926. During the boom period 1926–1929, private capital flowed into Austria and the other Central and Eastern European countries in considerable volume. Unfortunately, a large share of this credit was short-term. When U.S. bankers started to repatriate part of their investments to grant loans for profitable stock exchange speculation in 1928–1929, the fragility of the situation became apparent. Following the curtailment of capital exports from the United States after the crash of October 1929, the Creditanstalt, the foremost Austrian financial institution, had to absorb the Boden Creditanstalt, a large Austrian industrial and agricultural bank, on terms that represented a severe loss to the shareholders. The Creditanstalt, which found itself overburdened with nonperforming industrial loans, suffered a loss of $20 million in 1930, and on May 12, 1931, the Austrian government had to guarantee all deposits, foreign and domestic, of the bank in order to avert a breakdown of the banking system. The importance of the Creditanstalt affair lay less in the event than in its general significance. This is clearly shown in an appraisal made by the League of Nations in *Survey* 1932:

> It was instantly realized that, not only other banks in Austria and foreign countries, but virtually the whole industrial structure of Austria, and other Eastern European countries, would be involved. It was equally evident that neighbouring debtor states, and particularly Germany, would be at once exposed to the danger of panic withdrawals of capital. A crack had developed in the carefully constructed and patched facade of international finance and, through that crack, already timid investors and depositors caught glimpses of a weak and overburdened structure.[2]

Germany's economic revival in 1927–1929 was even more dependent on short-term foreign credit, as explained earlier. A Bank for International Settlements (BIS) committee estimated in a report of August 1931 that foreign investments in Germany totaled, at the end of 1930, Reichsmark (Rm) 25.5 billion (of which Rm 10.3 billion was short-term liabilities; Rm 1 = $0.24). German investments abroad totaled Rm 9.7 billion (of which Rm 4.5 billion was in short-term export credits and Rm 0.8 billion constituted all the foreign exchange of the Reichsbank; the remainder was long-term). Furthermore, this study showed, at the end of 1930, German banks had short-term liabilities amounting to Rm 7.2 billion and short-term assets of Rm 2.5 billion. Meanwhile exports of goods (including reparation deliveries in kind) amounted to Rm 12.1 billion in 1930 (14.5 percent of GNP). The committee noted that "there can be no doubt that the short-term credits of German banks have to a very large extent been used in the internal economy of Germany as working capital and therefore cannot be readily withdrawn without grave damage to the financial structure."[3] The fragility of the German financial system first became apparent in September 1930 when the Reichsbank suffered a run (due to the gravity of the internal political situation); securities were sold, and almost Rm 1 billion of foreign short-term credits were withdrawn. A loan from an international banking group temporarily stopped the run, but the Austro-German protocol of March 21, 1931, announcing the plan of a customs union (which violated the Versailles Treaty) strained international relations and made international economic cooperation more difficult. Soon after the announcement of the difficulties of the Creditanstalt, a renewed run began on the Reichsbank, which lost Rm 1 billion in four weeks. As in Austria, foreign transfers were followed by domestic runs on German banks. Germany announced on June 5, 1931, that it could not continue its reparations payments. On June 23, President Hoover proposed a one-year moratorium on reparations and war-debt payments, which became effective on July 6, 1931. The disclosure of enormous losses by the North-German Wool Company led to the closure of the Danat Bank on July 13, 1931. Other German banks were subjected to runs and imposed withdrawal limits of 5 to 20 percent of deposits. In the first seven months of 1931, foreign creditors withdrew Rm 2.9 billion from Germany, of which Rm 2.1 billion was short-term credits of the banks. The foreign banking groups concerned agreed between August 14 and 19, 1931, to continue extending credits to German debtors, up to the total then outstanding, for a period of six months. The agreement, which expired in February 1932, was renewed after prolonged negotiations, subject to the repayment of 10 percent of the outstanding total. Similar standstill agreements were signed with Austria and Hungary.

The Great Depression of 1929–1938

Even though the period 1925–1929 appeared to contemporaries as a time of prosperity, the politically powerful U.S. farm sector did not share in this prosperity, and the recovery of Central Europe was fragile, depending in large part on short-term financing from the United States, the United Kingdom, and France.

In 1925–1929, the United States dominated world manufacturing. In 1945, the League of Nations estimated that U.S. manufacturing production represented 42.5 percent of world manufacturing production, on average, over 1925–1929. The second largest producer was Germany (11.5 percent) followed by the United Kingdom (9.5 percent), France (6.6 percent), the USSR (4.0 percent), Italy (3.3 percent), Japan (2.5 percent), and Canada (2.4 percent). Together, the United States, Germany, the United Kingdom, and France accounted for 70.1 percent of world manufacturing production.

Trade statistics show a different distribution. Table 1.10 lists the average imports and exports of manufactured articles of the four leaders over several periods. In 1926–1929, the United Kingdom led the United States and Germany in exports, and France was a distant fourth. Essentially the United States, the world manufacturing giant, was supplying its domestic markets and exporting only a fraction of its production. But the United States was not independent of foreign economic upheavals in the interwar period (see Table 1.14 and especially Table 3.1), and both its balances on trade in merchandise and total trade in goods and services showed a surplus throughout the interwar period. On the other hand, the rest of the world was very dependent on the United States for commercial credits and industrial investments, and world prices had largely to adjust to U.S. prices. By the sheer weight of its economy, business cycles in the United States were propagated throughout international markets. This was apparent in 1921 when the sharp downturn in the U.S. economy was transmitted to the rest of the industrial countries with a one- to two-quarter lag; it was to be painfully obvious in 1929.

The total U.S. industrial production index (seasonally adjusted and including utilities) of the Federal Reserve Board reached a peak in the middle of 1929; after increasing by more than 15 percent in the twelve months ending June 1929, it stayed at the June level until August, fell by 12 percent from August to December, and remained almost stabilized in the first semester of 1930. It then fell by 16 percent from June to December 1930. According to the National Bureau of Economic Research (NBER), the overall economy peaked in August 1929. In summary, U.S. industry, after producing at a fairly constant level from early 1926 to mid-1928,

TABLE I.10 WORLD TRADE IN THE INTERWAR PERIOD
(TRADE IN MANUFACTURED ARTICLES ACCORDING TO
THE INTERNATIONAL [1913] CLASSIFICATION,
ANNUAL AVERAGES IN MILLIONS OF U.S. DOLLARS)

	1921–1925	*1926–1929*	*1930*	*1931–1935*	*1936–1938*
At 1913 prices					
United States					
Exports	784	1,267	1,115	685	1,116
Imports	448	665	530	372	444
Germany					
Exports	988	1,251	1,475	1,159	1,357
Imports	228	320	293	205	168
United Kingdom					
Exports	1,387	1,677	1,384	1,030	1,277
Imports	431	676	716	499	552
France					
Exports	729	848	765	574	409
Imports	187	210	337	245	179
In current prices					
United States					
Exports	1,436	2,027	1,686	629	862
Imports	821	1,064	773	342	343
Germany					
Exports	1,810	2,001	2,153	1,064	1,048
Imports	418	512	428	188	132
United Kingdom					
Exports	2,482	2,683	2,021	946	986
Imports	790	1,082	1,045	458	426
France					
Exports	1,336	1,356	1,117	527	316
Imports	342	336	492	225	138

SOURCE: League of Nations, *Industrialization and Foreign Trade* (Geneva, 1945), pp. 158, 160.

increased its output considerably in the following year before reducing it to the 1926–mid-1928 level by the end of 1929. It is clear that any explanation of the evolution of industrial output in the second half of 1929 must take into account the exceptional boom from mid-1928 to mid-1929 since the fall in output in the second half of 1929 almost appears to be a correction of the previous upward movement. Corporate profits after taxes—that is, aggregate dollar volume of profits after interest payments and corporate income taxes—increased by 15 percent from the second semester of 1927 to the first semester of 1928; they increased further from the first to the second semester of 1928 (by 29 percent) and in each of the two halves of 1929.[4] The stock exchange was frantic. The Dow Jones monthly average of industrial stocks rose by 41 percent from December 1927 to December 1928 and by 30 percent from December 1928 to September 1929. Finally, after realizing that industrial production had stopped growing in June 1929 due to the fairly tight monetary policy followed by the Federal Reserve Board, the stock market dramatically corrected itself in October and November 1929 *before rebounding* in December 1929 to a level that was still 25 percent above that of December 1927. The Dow kept increasing each month until April 1930, when it was *above* its December 1928 level. From mid-1930 until September 1930, the index fell relatively moderately. From September 1930 to June 1932, it dropped by 80 percent—its lowest point of the Depression.

The preceding paragraph leads to a crucial observation: the upward phase in industrial activity, profits, and the stock exchange from mid-1928 to mid-1929 corrected itself in the second half of 1929 to levels stabilized in the first quarter (and almost the entire first semester) of 1930, at or above the levels of 1928. In other words, up to mid-1930 there existed a business cycle essentially similar to most business cycles. But industrial output fell in the second quarter of 1930 (production was probably reduced to cut existing stocks[5]). Confidence was shattered in the third quarter (if the stock exchange is an index of confidence), and the economy dropped precipitously until the first semester of 1933. It appears that a determined effort by monetary and fiscal authorities in the first semester of 1930 and possibly as late as the summer of 1930 could have avoided the collapse of the economy.

As discussed above, the U.S. economy totally dominated the world economy, and the United States enjoyed a surplus in its international trade of goods and services of more than a billion dollars every year from 1927 to 1930 (the GNP in 1930 was $90.7 billion). President Hoover chose this moment to sign into law, on June 17, 1930, one of the largest tariff increases in international trade history.

If the Hawley-Smoot Tariff dealt a huge blow to international business confidence and the international economy, it was only one of two devastating policy mistakes of the U. S. authorities. The NBER dates the trough of the Depression to March 1933 for the overall economy. From the cyclical peak of economic activity in August 1929 to the cyclical trough in March 1933, the stock of money fell by over a third. Milton Friedman and Anna Schwartz, in their *Monetary History of the United States*, have correctly judged that this dramatic reduction in the stock of money was one of the major causes of the Depression. What is less known, however, is that the stock of money (both M1 and M2) went almost unchanged from January 1928 until April 1930 and fell only marginally until March 1931 (from April 1930 to March 1931, M1 decreased by 4 percent and M2 by 3 percent). Then, from March 1931 to March 1933, M1 contracted by 22 percent and M2 by 30 percent.

To summarize, the failure of the Federal Reserve to increase, as would have been rational, the quantity of money in a noninflationary economy experiencing strong real growth terminated, in mid-1929, the upward phase of the 1928 business cycle. The economy adapted itself to the constant money stock by correcting the upward movement in the downturn of the second half of 1929. The economy was stabilized in the first half of 1930 at a level appropriate to the stock of money. But the Hawley-Smoot Tariff destabilized the world economy in June 1930. It precipitated the crisis in Central Europe that led to the financial crises of 1931 and to the devaluation of the pound sterling in September 1931, aggravating the world depression, which the United States could not control after mid-1930. The United States could have limited the extent of the Depression by stabilizing its stock of money after March 1931. Instead the Federal Reserve allowed the U.S. financial system to collapse.

The impact of the Depression on the GDP and industrial production of the four major industrial countries of the time is fully apparent in Tables 1.1–1.4. The United States and Germany suffered most; French industrial output was the last to fall but never recovered during the remainder of the period; the United Kingdom suffered least of all.

INTERNATIONAL FINANCIAL FLOWS AND EXCHANGE RATE POLICIES

After World War I, there was a general return of currencies to the gold standard. The mark was stabilized in 1924, and the British pound returned to its prewar parity on April 28, 1925. Most of the Central and Eastern European currencies returned to gold between 1924 and 1928. After being stabilized in 1927, the French franc was officially devalued on June 25, 1928, and gold convertibility was restored. By the end of the 1920s, the main world currencies were linked by fixed exchange rates. But the restored gold standard differed from the prewar system; the new system was a gold exchange standard based on the recommendations of the Genoa conference of 1922, which had met to organize monetary reconstruction. Under the gold exchange standard, the international reserves of most countries consisted largely of sterling or dollar balances backed by gold instead of consisting of gold itself, as under a gold standard. This meant that large amounts of sterling and dollar balances could be shifted from one financial center to another as expectations and business confidence changed. These international capital flows could destroy, at any time, the weakest link in the chain of reserve currencies. At the end of the 1920s, financial markets perceived sterling as the weak link.

The opposition of many economists, especially Keynes, to the return of sterling to its prewar parity is well known. To contemporary observers, the overvaluation of the pound between 1925 and 1931 was one of the main reasons for high British unemployment. But British national income accounts, reconstituted after World War II, show that the economic situation was not as disastrous as contemporaries believed. After an initial period of adjustment, the British GDP (see Table 1.2) increased by 11 percent from 1926 to 1929, and the average annual growth rate over the period 1925–1929 was 2.1 percent. By comparison, net national income grew, on average, by 1.1 percent per annum between 1900 and 1913 and by 2.1 percent per annum between 1920 and 1938. So the 1925–1929 era, marked by a supposedly overvalued pound sterling (before the British economy was hit by the Depression), saw a real growth rate equal to that of the interwar period and much superior to the prewar growth rate. If industrial production fell in 1926, its rebound in 1927 was extraordinary (see Table 1.2).

The British current account was equally strong. The current balance (see Table 1.11) showed a total surplus of £234 million over the period 1926–1930 during a time of a supposedly overvalued pound sterling and a deficit of £112 million over the period 1932–1934, after the large devaluation of 1931. But contemporary observers emphasized the trade deficit in the late 1920s.

Contemporary observers were very aware of the unemployment statistics and the declining fortunes of the major export-oriented industries, such as coal, cotton, and shipbuilding, and did not perceive in the absence of national income and complete balance-of-payments statistics, the growth of new industries and services that supplied essentially domestic markets.

Modern explanations of the high unemployment in interwar Britain emphasize the extremely generous unemployment benefits relative to British wages and relative to insurance schemes in other industrial countries. Brian Kantor, in a review of the modern literature, concludes that "the unemployment benefit policy, associated as it was with structural changes in the British economy, seriously inhibited the mobility of labor to areas where industrial expansion occurred. The effect of the policy was to be seen in high levels of measured unemployment and increases in real wages."[6]

Although the British economy was sound and strong in 1927–1929 and held out well against the Great Depression in 1930 (see Table 1.2), two reports disturbed business confidence in 1931. Britain, as is normal for the leading financial center, had large short-term foreign assets and liabilities. On July 13, 1931, the Macmillan report drew attention to the volume of short-term claims on London, and on July 31, 1931, the May report predicted a substantial budget deficit unless the Labour government curtailed

TABLE 1.11   BRITISH CURRENT ACCOUNTS, 1920–1938
            (IN MILLIONS OF POUNDS)

	Trade balance	Services balance	Current balance
1920	− 148	+ 463	+ 315
1921	− 148	+ 322	+ 174
1922	− 63	+ 244	+ 181
1923	− 97	+ 259	+ 162
1924	− 214	+ 272	+ 58
1925	− 265	+ 296	+ 31
1926	− 346	+ 307	− 39
1927	− 270	+ 348	+ 78
1928	− 237	+ 341	+ 104
1929	− 263	+ 339	+ 76
1930	− 283	+ 298	+ 15
1931	− 322	+ 208	− 114
1932	− 216	+ 154	− 62
1933	− 192	+ 174	− 18
1934	− 220	+ 188	− 32
1935	− 183	+ 196	+ 13
1936	− 263	+ 223	− 40
1937	− 336	+ 279	− 57
1938	− 285	+ 220	− 65

SOURCE: Richard S. Sayers, *The Bank of England, 1891–1944*, vol. 12 (Cambridge, Eng.: Cambridge University Press, 1976).

expenditures. At the time, British bankers were heavily involved in Central Europe. For example, a BIS committee reported that, as of March 31, 1931, out of a total of Rm 5.6 billion of short-term liabilities of the leading German banks, 37.1 percent was due to the United States and 20.4 percent to Britain. With the financial crisis in Central Europe and especially Germany, a large amount of British short-term credit rapidly became frozen in July–August 1931. As a consequence of these factors, over £200 million (£1 = $4.86) was withdrawn from the London money market in the two months preceding September 20, 1931. Although the Bank of England raised its discount rate from 2.5 to 3.5 percent on July 23 and to 4.5 percent a week later, it made no further adjustment until after September 21. It appears that British currency was ill-defended in those crucial days. While the Bank of England supported the pound extensively with the aid of foreign credits, it held on to its gold reserve until almost the devaluation and did not allow the currency to fall to the gold export point. But most important, the Bank of England did not use the discount rate, which was raised to 6 percent after the devaluation, to defend the pound in August and September.

A supplementary budget imposing heavier taxation was introduced on

September 10, 1931, but five days later, a protest in the Atlantic Fleet against pay reduction received wide publicity and frightened financial markets. Between Wednesday morning, September 16, and Saturday noon, September 19, over £43 million of short-term funds was withdrawn. The decision was made on the nineteenth to let sterling float, and on September 21, 1931, Parliament approved legislation suspending the Bank of England's obligation to sell gold. Exchange rates with respect to gold currencies dropped 25 percent almost immediately. The National Government, formed on August 24, 1931, received an overwhelming majority in the elections of October 27, 1931, and the budget was balanced. What appeared as a new beginning for Britain, however, was to be a major cause of the deepening of the international depression. Most of the countries in close financial relationship with Great Britain abandoned the gold standard in the following months. Before the end of October 1931, all the British Dominions, except South Africa, and the rest of the British empire, as well as the Scandinavian and several other countries, had departed from gold. Japan followed in December 1931.

The breakdown of the international financial system put immense pressure on the remaining gold standard countries, whose currencies became overvalued with respect to their foremost competitor. When Britain went off gold, all the European stock exchanges, except those of Paris, Milan, and Prague, closed for various periods; bank rates rose; 30 countries imposed foreign exchange restrictions (ranging from limitations of imports to moratoriums); and many countries increased tariffs or introduced contingent, priority, and quota systems.

The storm center, which had shifted from Austria to Germany in May 1931 and to Britain in August–September 1931, now shifted back to the United States, where the world crisis had begun. In September–October 1931, a "gold rush" set in and reduced U.S. gold stocks by $725 million. Those losses brought the gold stock back to its average level of 1929. The Federal Reserve System, which had let the internal banking crisis develop, reacted vigorously to the external drain. The Reserve Bank of New York raised its rediscount rate to 2.5 percent on October 9, and to 3.5 percent on October 16—"the sharpest rise within so brief a period in the whole history of the System, before or since."[7] (Chapter 2 discusses the monetary crises in greater detail.) This move intensified the internal financial difficulties: the number of bank failures and runs on banks increased sharply.

All told, in the six months from August 1931 through January 1932, 1,860 banks with deposits of $1,449 million suspended operations, and the deposits of those banks that managed to keep afloat fell by a much larger sum. Total deposits fell over the six-month period by nearly five times the deposits in suspended banks or by no less than 17 percent of the initial level of deposits in operating banks . . . Why should the gold drain and the subsequent rise in discount rates have intensified the domestic financial difficulties so greatly? They would not have done so, if they had been accompanied by extensive open market purchases designed to offset the effect of the external gold drain on high-powered money, and of the internal currency drain on bank reserves. Unfortunately, purchases were not made . . . The result was that the banks found their reserves being drained from two directions—by export of gold and by internal demands for currency.[8]

The U.S. financial system finally crashed in March 1933. As noted above, from the cyclical peak of the economy's output in August 1929 to the cyclical trough in March 1933, the stock of money fell by over a third. President Roosevelt's proclamation of a bank holiday on March 6, 1933, also froze the gold stocks of the private banking sector. Then, on April 20, 1933, the United States suspended the operation of the gold standard through an executive order prohibiting the export of gold. At the end of April 1933, the dollar had fallen to a discount of 10 percent in Paris, France being the last remaining major power to maintain the gold standard.

On June 12, 1933, the major industrial powers convened the World Economic and Monetary Conference in London. On July 8, 1933, when it had become clear that the conference would reach no generally acceptable conclusions regarding immediate world monetary policy, representatives of the central banks of France, Belgium, Italy, the Netherlands, Poland, and Switzerland met in Paris at the request of their respective governments and drew up a protocol providing for the common defense of the gold standard. An immediate result was the subsidizing of active speculation against the Dutch florin and the Swiss franc.

On January 30, 1934, Roosevelt signed the Gold Reserve Act, redefining the gold content of the U.S. dollar and re-establishing a gold standard in the United States. The price of gold was fixed on January 31, 1934, at $35 per fine ounce, a depreciation of 40.94 percent.

The countries that decided to maintain the gold standard (the "gold bloc") experienced a deepening of the Depression after the fall of the pound sterling in 1931; their difficulties increased in the spring of 1933 after the floating of the dollar, when speculation against their currencies developed. France resisted the necessary devaluation. After four years of deflation, the Popular Front, elected in April-May 1936, reflated massively in June while maintaining the commitment to the gold standard. The system exploded, and the franc was devalued tardily and insufficiently on October 1, 1936. On June 30, 1937, the French government took the franc off the gold standard and let it float.

The case of Germany, one of the four major industrial powers, was different. By 1931, Germany had achieved a trade surplus by greatly reducing its imports while maintaining its exports, and its only balance-of-payments problems originated in the flight of capital. But even after Britain left the gold standard, Germany did not devalue since in the public mind, devaluation and inflation were inseparably connected. Foreign exchange controls, instituted in July 1931, became permanent in November 1931. Berlin attempted deflation in December 1931, with little clear result. In order to maintain external equilibrium, Germany resorted for the remainder of the 1930s to import licensing, control of foreign payments on loan account, and bilateral trading arrangements.

The failure of the World Economic and Monetary Conference in June–July 1933 marked the end of an era. It was the last international economic conference before the war and the last major effort to cope with economic problems internationally. When it was finally realized that there were no national solutions to the crisis, the United States, the United Kingdom, and France agreed at the end of September 1936 that exchange rates should not be changed without prior consultation.[9] A sort of variable gold standard had been restored.

It bears emphasizing that attempts by several major countries, starting with Great Britain, to solve their problems nationally by competitive devaluation only led to a deepening of the Depression in all countries, except for short periods when some countries enjoyed a relative devaluation advantage. The small undervaluation of the franc after 1928 and the lack of strong and determined international cooperation in 1931 (beyond credits) did not help the British. While the Central European financial crisis was the proximate cause of the fall of the pound sterling, it is clear that London did not firmly resist the devaluation, which influential groups had been urging since 1925. A 10 percent formal devaluation of the pound to re-establish purchasing power parity,[10] coupled with strong action on the part of the Bank of England and full international cooperation, would have solved the British problem and contained the financial crisis to Central Europe. Britain had the strength to resist, but the lack of adequate information and an abundance of poor economic thinking undermined its will.

INTERNATIONAL TRADE

Table 1.12 illustrates two important facts about international trade in the period considered: first, the price index of the composite good representative of all goods traded fell by 12 percent from 1925 to 1929, while the volume or quantum index increased by 20 percent. This points to an ongoing

TABLE 1.12   WORLD TRADE: VALUE, PRICE, AND QUANTUM, ANNUAL FIGURES, 1913–1938

| | RECORDED VALUE Old U.S. gold $ (millions) | | TOTAL (in millions) | | VALUE INDEX (1929 = 100) | | PRICE INDEX (1929 = 100) | | QUANTUM INDEX (1929 = 100) |
	Imports	Exports	Gold $	£	Gold $	£	Gold $	£	
1913	21,034	19,564	40,598	8,342	59.2	59.2	(73.5)*	(73.5)*	
1924	28,978	27,850	56,828	12,865	82.8	91.2	109.4	120.5	75.7
1925	33,150	31,551	64,701	13,295	94.3	94.3	113.4	113.4	83.2
1926	32,117	29,920	62,037	12,747	90.4	90.4	106.1	106.1	85.2
1927	33,764	31,516	65,280	13,414	95.1	95.1	103.5	103.5	91.9
1928	34,652	32,728	67,380	13,845	98.2	98.2	103.1	103.1	95.2
1929	35,595	33,024	68,619	14,100	100.0	100.0	100.0	100.0	100.0
1930	29,075	26,477	55,552	11,415	81.0	81.0	87.1	87.1	93.0
1931	20,795	18,906	39,701	8,754	57.9	62.1	67.7	72.6	85.5
1932	13,968	12,885	26,853	7,659	39.1	54.3	52.4	72.7	74.6
1933	12,461	11,714	24,175	7,295	35.2	51.7	46.7	68.6	75.4
1934	11,981	11,333	23,314	7,757	34.0	55.0	43.5	70.4	78.2
1935	12,243	11,559	23,802	8,182	34.7	58.0	42.4	70.9	81.8
1936	13,142	12,581	25,723	8,744	37.5	62.0	43.7	72.3	85.8
1937	16,342	15,427	31,769	10,880	46.3	77.2	48.0	80.0	96.5
1938	14,319	13,417	27,736	9,604	40.4	68.1	45.5	76.7	88.8

SOURCE: League of Nations, World Trade Series, 1939.
*Indicative.

situation of oversupply and extreme competition in world markets. Second, in value terms, international trade peaked in 1929 at 69 percent above its level of 1913; then it collapsed completely between 1929 and 1933 and essentially stayed at a level roughly two-thirds below the 1929 level until the end of the period, except for a limited one-year recovery in 1937. Table 1.13 shows that all categories of goods participated in the collapse of international trade since the deviation around the mean in 1933 is very small.

A further fact is that, as might be expected, the prices of primary commodities such as foodstuffs and raw materials fell much more than the prices of manufactured articles. In other words, the terms of trade shifted in favor of the industrial countries.

Table 1.14 illustrates another aspect of the situation. The value of exports fell much more than the value of output for each of the major powers. This meant that the sector producing internationally traded goods in each economy suffered more from the crisis than the sector producing nontraded goods. Since the traded-goods sector is usually the most dynamic and innovative sector in an economy, the world economy regressed even more in terms of technological progress and efficiency than can be inferred from the overall statistics. Obviously, these developments are explained by the trade war, which raised barriers to international trade.

The U.S. Hawley-Smoot Tariff became effective on June 17, 1930, and was the signal for an outburst of tariff-making activity in other countries. The second phase of the tariff war started with the British devaluation in September 1931. Although Britain benefited from a devaluation of about 30 percent, the Abnormal Importations Act, passed on November 19, 1931, gave the Board of Trade discretionary powers to impose duties ranging up to 100 percent. On the day the bill passed, the board issued an order fixing a 50 percent duty on 23 classes of goods; other orders followed. These orders were directed primarily at the European competitors of Great Britain, especially Germany. The new duties were very effective, and imports of the affected commodities practically ceased. Then, on March 1, 1932, Britain imposed a 10 percent general tariff increase. In July 1932, the Ottawa Conference provided for empire preference; the British Dominions were instructed to grant preferences to British goods, and very restrictive quotas were applied to Japanese textiles. The same demand was made on other countries dependent on the British market.

Germany resorted to import licensing and bilateral trading arrangements in November 1931. These restrictions were stiffened several times throughout the period. By 1934, exchange control and import licensing were linked with economic planning.

The average French tariff rate fell from 15 percent in 1928 to 12 percent in 1930. In November 1931, an exchange surtax of 15 percent ad valorem was applied on British goods. But from mid-1931 on, the French resorted essentially to quotas to restrict imports. By 1936, 65 percent of French imports came under the quota system.

Indeed, throughout the period, two trends emerged in the evolution of international trade. First, trade became bilateral or regional within existing empires. Second, tariff restrictions were increasingly complemented by administrative measures, such as prohibitions, quotas, licensing systems, and clearing agreements. By the mid-1930s, international trade had become, in large proportion, barter trade. As a consequence, the benefits of multilateral trade were lost, and the effects of comparative advantage wasted. This compounded the overall loss of efficiency due to the retrenchment of the traded-goods sector of the world economy. Tables 1.12 and 1.14 illustrate the inanity of protectionist measures. Protectionism only led to a reduction of international trade, affecting all trading nations to a comparable extent, whether they initiated the trade war or merely retaliated. A major trading nation gains nothing but a temporary advantage in introducing restrictions, and in the end it pays a permanently high cost for its misguided policy. It is clear that the collapse of international trade in the Depression made international recovery virtually impossible for a decade.

THE EVENTS LEADING TO THE CRISIS IN THE UNITED STATES

The Great Depression in the United States was not one event from 1929 to 1938; it consisted of three distinct episodes: a business cycle from mid-1928 to mid-1930, with economic activity reaching its peak in August 1929; an ever accelerating fall of economic activity initiated by the Hawley-Smoot Tariff in June 1930, ending in the collapse of the financial system in the first semester of 1933; and a recovery that was checked by misguided economic policies. (The next chapter reviews the monetary aspects of the second and the third episodes.)

The United States dominated the international economy in 1925–1929, producing 42.5 percent of world industrial output, but its business cycles were transmitted more by price (including interest) movements and by capital flows and international investments than by trade in goods and services: U.S. industry primarily supplied its domestic market. The U.S. business cycle of 1928–1930 was essentially characterized by a constant stock of money. Indeed, M1 went almost unchanged from the third quarter of 1925 to the first quarter of 1930, and M2 increased by 8 percent from the third quarter of 1925 to the first quarter of 1928, remaining roughly unchanged until the first quarter of 1930. U.S. industrial output, which was

PERCENTAGE SHARE IN THE VALUE OF WORLD TRADE

	Foodstuffs	Raw materials*	Manufactured articles	Total
1929	24.5	36.0	39.5	100
1930	25.5	34.5	40.0	100
1931	27.5	32.5	40.0	100
1932	29.0	33.0	38.0	100
1933	26.5	36.0	37.5	100
1934	25.0	37.0	38.0	100
1935	24.5	37.5	38.0	100
1936	24.5	38.0	37.5	100
1937	23.0	39.5	37.5	100
1938	24.0	36.0	40.0	100

MOVEMENT OF VALUE (IN GOLD) (1929 = 100)

	Foodstuffs	Raw materials*	Manufactured articles	Total
1929	100.0	100.0	100.0	100.0
1930	83.0	77.5	83.0	81.0
1931	63.5	52.5	59.5	57.9
1932	46.5	38.0	37.5	39.1
1933	37.5	35.0	34.0	35.2
1934	34.0	35.0	33.0	34.0
1935	34.5	36.0	33.5	34.7
1936	37.0	39.5	36.0	37.5
1937	43.0	51.0	44.5	46.3
1938	39.5	40.5	41.5	40.5

PRICE MOVEMENTS (IN GOLD) (1929 = 100)

	Foodstuffs	Raw materials*	Manufactured articles	Total
1929	100.0	100.0	100.0	100.0
1930	84.5	82.0	94.0	87.1
1931	66.5	59.0	78.0	67.7
1932	52.0	44.0	63.5	52.4
1933	45.5	40.0	56.5	46.7
1934	41.5	39.5	50.0	43.5

QUANTUM MOVEMENTS (1929 = 100)

	Foodstuffs	Raw materials*	Manufactured articles	Total
1929	100.0	100.0	100.0	100.0
1930	98.0	94.5	88.0	93.0
1931	96.0	88.5	76.0	85.5
1932	89.0	81.5	59.5	74.6
1933	83.0	87.5	60.0	75.4
1934	82.0	88.0	66.5	78.2

1935	40.5	39.0	48.0	42.4	85.5	92.5	69.5	81.8
1936	42.0	41.5	48.0	43.7	88.0	95.5	75.0	85.8
1937	45.5	47.0	51.0	48.0	93.5	108.0	87.0	96.5
1938	43.0	42.5	50.5	45.5	91.5	95.0	82.0	88.8

SOURCE: League of Nations, World Trade Series, 1939.

NOTE: The distinction between the three groups is drawn in accordance with the International (Brussels, 1913) classification, "live animals" being included with foodstuffs. The price movement was estimated on the basis of figures available for five principal trading countries (the United Kingdom, the United States, Germany, France, and Italy). Since up-to-date information concerning the distribution of trade by groups is available only for a limited number of countries, the figures for 1938 must be regarded as tentative estimates.

*Including "materials, partly manufactured."

TABLE 1.14   SHARE OF EXPORTS OF GOODS IN GNP, 1929–1938

	United States	United Kingdom	Germany	France
1929	5.1	14.2	14.4	13.9
1930	4.3	11.5	14.5	12.0
1931	3.3	8.7	13.8	9.0
1932	2.9	8.2	10.4	6.5
1933	3.0	8.1	8.5	6.3
1934	3.4	8.4	6.3	6.8
1935	3.3	8.5	5.8	6.0
1936	3.1	7.5	5.8	5.3
1937	3.9	9.2	6.4	6.8
1938	3.8	8.2	5.1	7.1

SOURCE: Author's calculations from League of Nations and countries' national accounts.

fairly constant from early 1926 to mid-1928, increased considerably in the following year before being cut to its 1926–mid-1928 level by the end of 1929; it stabilized at roughly its December 1929 level in the first quarter (and almost the entire first semester) of 1930. More generally, and due to the tight monetary policy followed by the Federal Reserve Board, the upward phase in industrial activity, profits, and the stock exchange from mid-1928 to mid-1929 corrected itself in the second half of 1929 to levels stabilized in the first quarter (and almost the entire first semester) of 1930 at or above the levels of 1928.

If U.S. monetary policy had been more expansionary in the first and especially the second quarters of 1930, the business cycle of 1928–1930 and the stock market crash of 1929 would be known only to specialists. But the Federal Reserve tightened its grip at a time when a very confused U.S. administration delivered a major blow to the international economy: on June 17, 1930, President Hoover signed into law a major tariff increase. Furthermore, due to the domestic financial situation, U.S. net outflows of private capital (representing changes in assets or in investments of the U.S. private sector abroad and not covering changes in liabilities of the U.S. private sector to residents of foreign countries) fell from $1,541 million in 1928 to $836 and $555 million in 1929 and 1930, respectively, and turned into capital inflows of $56 million in 1931 and $478 million in 1932.[11] This further aggravated the financial crisis of the overexposed Central European banking system: U.S. refinancing of the large short-term liabilities of the Central European economies was cut at precisely the time when what became rapidly a raging international trade war reduced their actual and anticipated foreign earnings. The ensuing financial crisis in Central Europe was the proximate cause of the devaluation of the British pound. The trade war redoubled, and the international economy disintegrated in the incredible course of three short years. In the same period of 1930–1933, the direct and indirect consequences of the collapse of the international economy speeded the crash, unchecked by the authorities, of the U.S. financial system. In an environment of a disintegrating domestic financial system and international economy, the activity of the immensely powerful and efficient U.S. manufacturing sector came to a halt: U.S. industrial output was cut in half from mid-1929 to mid-1932 and remained at that level until the first quarter of 1933. World manufacturing output fell by 29 percent from 1929 to 1932.

The downward phase of the 1928–1930 business cycle was caused by a tight U.S. monetary policy, the trade war was started by the U.S. Congress and president, the crash of the U.S. financial system was not checked by the U.S. Federal Reserve, the overvaluation and later devaluation at the worst possible moment of the pound sterling was the responsibility of the British government, and the trade war of the 1930s was conducted by all the well-meaning governments of the world. However, most of the literature on the Great Depression, except for a few seminal studies, has dealt with the internal weaknesses of the private productive sector or the insufficient effective demand of the household sector. But if the Federal Reserve had pumped money into the system in the second quarter of 1930 and kept the money stock slightly increasing thereafter and if Hoover had vetoed the Hawley-Smoot Tariff in June 1930, there would probably not have been a Great Depression.

2

Interwar Monetary and Fiscal Policies in the United States, France, and the United Kingdom

Four countries dominated the world manufacturing economy in the interwar period: the United States, Germany, Great Britain, and France, in that order. Only three of these countries, the United States, Great Britain, and France (after 1927), had the financial strength to pursue partly independent policies that could affect the rest of the world. Germany, on the other hand, did not start recovering from the hyperinflation of 1922–1923 until 1926 and depended on the rest of the world; its prosperity in 1926–1929 was largely financed by foreign short-term borrowing. Indeed, when, in 1930–1931, these loans were called in, the country plunged into a recession aggravated by the loss of its export markets due to the trade war. Then, through import licensing and bilateral trade agreements supplemented by a very strict exchange control system, Germany isolated itself from the rest of the world. The United Kingdom and France, partly thanks to their empires, and the United States, by the sheer weight of its economy, were the three main decisionmakers in 1927–1936.

Germany and Japan, in the 1930s, and the Soviet Union, since the revolution, had planned economies; the first two countries recovered well from the crisis, and the last one largely escaped the Great Depression; by asserting their renewed economic and military strength, they joined the three democracies in shaping world history after 1936. But in the decade 1927–1936, the three democracies and future allies exercised their political and military domination over the world, and their monetary and fiscal policies shaped the evolution of the international economy.

MONETARY POLICIES

From 1925 to 1931, the United Kingdom essentially used monetary policy to maintain the exchange rate. Since the United States was following a tight monetary policy, the United Kingdom had no choice but to adapt to it in order to maintain the dollar-pound parity. After September 1931, British money stocks were allowed to increase, and the banking system never lost the confidence of the public. Since budget deficits were relatively small and the economy was adequately financed, the private sector did not have to compete with the public sector to get loans: the average growth rate of the British economy over the period 1929–1938 is spectacular compared with those of the United States and France. Especially remarkable is the small reduction in British output over the period 1930–1934: Great Britain essentially escaped the Great Depression. By contrast, the United States and France followed destabilizing monetary policies.

The United States

As emphasized above, M1 (currency held by the public plus demand deposits at commercial banks) went almost unchanged from the third quarter of 1925 to the first quarter of 1930, while M2 (M1 plus time deposits at commercial banks) increased by 8 percent from the third quarter of 1925 to the first quarter of 1928 and then remained roughly unchanged until the first quarter of 1930. Since consumer prices (taken as representative of the GDP deflator) were essentially stable from 1927 to 1929, the real quantity of money (the stock of money divided by the price index) went almost unchanged from 1927 to 1929. To accommodate the increase in real activity in that period, the velocity of money had to rise substantially. Since there are institutional limits to the rise in velocity, the economy was starved for liquidity and soon retreated to a lower level of output.

Business confidence was shaken by passage of the Hawley-Smoot Tariff in June 1930. Then, in November 1930, a series of bank failures led to widespread attempts to convert demand and time deposits into currency. Bank failures increased, and some large banks had to suspend operations in December. The crisis did not last long, and both M1 and M2 were stabilized or slightly increased in the first quarter of 1931. By then, industrial production had fallen by a third and the stock exchange index by a half from the peaks of 1929, and the international trade war was raging. After March 1931, "the public resumed converting deposits into currency, and from April on, banks started strengthening their reserve position, liquidating available assets in order to meet both the public's demand for currency and their own desire for liquidity." Meanwhile, the financial crisis in Central Europe further weakened the international monetary system: "The failure of world-famous financial institutions and the widespread closing of banks in a great country could not but render depositors throughout the world uneasy and enhance the desire of bankers everywhere to strengthen their positions."[1]

The international financial crisis culminated in the devaluation of sterling on September 21, 1931. The storm center moved to New York, and the Federal Reserve had to take strong action to defend the dollar (see Chapter 1); this worsened domestic financial difficulties. The stock price index reached its lowest point in June 1932 (an 87 percent decline since September 1929), in unison with the industrial production index (a 53 percent drop from August 1929 to July 1932). The trade war was raging; wholesale prices were plummeting (see Table 1.1). U.S. farmers were harvesting the effects of the tariff they had wanted: the ratio of prices received for all farm products to prices paid fell by a third from 1929 to 1932 (see Table 1.6). There were many bank failures in the last quarter of 1932 in the rural Midwest and Far West. The situation worsened quickly, and by March 3, 1933, about half the states had declared banking holidays, relieving banks of the necessity to meet their obligations to creditors. President Roosevelt proclaimed a nationwide banking holiday after midnight on March 6, which lasted until March 13, 14, or 15, depending on the location of the bank. From the cyclical peak of activity in August 1929 to the cyclical trough in March 1933, the stock of money fell by over a third.

The inability of U.S. monetary authorities to check the banking system failure contributed to its spread and to the huge decrease in bank deposits and money supply; one naturally wonders why the Federal Reserve System did not intervene to help the banking system by initiating the required open-market operations and to increase as much as was needed the liquidity of banks—both were operations that it was empowered to conduct. At the time, the Federal Reserve Board relied in its day-to-day operations on the *real-bills doctrine* (monetary policy should be conducted to provide credit in response to the "needs of trade"). As summarized by Allan Meltzer in a study of the causes of the Great Depression, "If market interest rates rose and the rise was accompanied by an increase in loans eligible for discount at the central bank—real bills—a central bank operating according to the doctrine permitted borrowing to increase. The stocks of money and bank credit rose in periods of economic expansion and declined in recessions."[2] This is precisely what happened in the United States during the Depression. By focusing on interest rates and on the apparent liquidity of member-banks of the Federal Reserve System while completely ignoring the dynamics of runs on banks, the Federal Reserve watched several waves of runs on banks until March 1933 with little reaction. Few contemporary commentators criticized this policy. Some wrongly considered that the Federal Reserve lacked the power to act.

The 1933 Banking Act established the federal insurance of bank deposits, and the 1935 Banking Act increased the powers of what became the Board of Governors of the Federal Reserve System (instead of the Federal

Reserve Board) to change reserve requirements, limit interest rates, and regulate banks. With the devaluation of the dollar and establishment of the deposit insurance system in 1933, confidence returned and the stock of money increased sharply in 1934–1936, contributing to the recovery of output.

France

As usual, France followed a policy opposite to that of the United States and Great Britain. Surprisingly (given French economic management in the 1930s), French monetary policy was at first much more reasonable than the Anglo-Saxon variety.

Poincaré stabilized the franc in 1927 and devalued it de jure in June 1928, by 80 percent from the prewar gold parity. As mentioned earlier, Keynes thought this a smart move. With the implicit write-off of debts and the return of confidence, the French economy boomed and proved resilient to the Depression until 1931. Not surprisingly, the money stock increased in France until 1931. France was a refuge for international capital at a time of great uncertainty in Britain and the United States. M1 actually increased at an annual rate of 12 percent from the third to the fourth quarter of 1931, after the British devaluation, and, on average, the stock of money was almost exactly constant from 1931 to 1932 (Table 1.3 gives end-of-year stocks). The stock of money was only 2 percent below the 1931–32 average in the first three quarters of 1933. The devaluation of the dollar, which had been limited until June, increased considerably in July 1933 and reached 37 percent with respect to the French franc in November 1933. The franc appeared overvalued, some outflows of capital were registered, and the French themselves started to convert their deposits into currency and began hoarding gold. The French government stepped up its deflationary policies, and from the third quarter of 1933 to the first quarter of 1936, M1 fell by 5.4 percent and M2 by 5.1 percent. The Socialist government, which came to power in the second quarter of 1936, started to borrow heavily from the Central Bank in the third quarter. Due to large outflows of capital, the net effect was a marginal reduction in the stock of money. The franc was finally devalued on October 1, 1936. From the third quarter of 1936 to the second quarter of 1939, M1 increased by 49.5 percent and M2 by 38 percent, with the inflationary consequences recorded in Table 1.3.

Quite naturally, the reduction in the stock of money in 1933–1936 at a time of heavy public borrowing from the private sector to finance ever increasing budget deficits starved the productive sector of funds; at that time the British were pursuing precisely the opposite policy. As a consequence of French monetary policy, real activity in France remained stagnant throughout the period 1931–1936 and was especially depressed in 1934–1936—during the worldwide recovery.

Contrary to what has been taught to generations of students and future policymakers, government policies—whether active, such as trade policies (increased tariffs), or passive, such as monetary policies (the failure of U.S. monetary authorities to intervene and check the collapse of the financial system)—started the Great Depression. Despite what is usually taught and still repeated today, monetary policy used wisely in conjunction with a restrained fiscal policy proved to be the most powerful policy instrument to stabilize a capitalist economy.

Fiscal Policies and Regulatory Practices

The only country that resisted the Great Depression well, the United Kingdom, had a budget almost in balance. Both the United States and France experienced large budget deficits. Tables 2.1–2.3 present the administrative budgets of these three countries.

The evolution of fiscal expenditures and deficits cannot be taken as a test of the efficacy of fiscal policy in the United States since the collapse of the financial system was the primary cause of the reduction in output while the recovery of the financial system after 1933 largely accounted for the return to a normal activity. But the pre-eminence of monetary policy is confirmed by the observation that fiscal policy was strongly expansionary as early as 1931, to no avail, while the reduction in government expenditures and in the deficit in 1935 did not check the recovery.

In France, the share of the deficit in expenditures increased from around 10 percent in 1930–1932 to 20 percent in 1933–1935 to above 30 percent in 1936–1938. The deficit in 1930–1935 was financed for the most part by borrowing while the stock of money was falling in 1933–1935. Huge public borrowings in credit markets that were getting narrower and narrower crowded out the private sector: there is evidence of credit rationing in 1934–1935 (see the annual studies of the *Revue d'Economie Politique*). The lack of loanable funds checked the two recoveries of French economic activity during the Great Depression (August 1932–July 1933 and December 1935–April 1936). If French authorities had let the franc float in the second quarter of 1933, the country would have experienced a recovery comparable to the one in Britain since the stock of money would have been stabilized or would have risen as confidence was being restored. Instead the French government resorted to forced cuts in prices and spending, which only exacerbated an already volatile political situation.

TABLE 2.1   U.S. GOVERNMENT FINANCES
(ADMINISTRATIVE BUDGETS), 1919–1939
FEDERAL GOVERNMENT
(IN BILLIONS OF DOLLARS)

	FISCAL YEAR ENDING JUNE				
	Receipts	*Expenditures*	*Surplus or deficit (−)*	*Total public debt*	GDP CURRENT PRICES
1919	5.13	18.49	−13.36	25.48	
1920	6.65	6.36	0.29	24.30	
1921	5.57	5.06	0.51	23.98	
1922	4.03	3.29	0.74	22.96	
1923	3.85	3.14	0.71	22.35	
1924	3.87	2.91	0.96	21.25	
1925	3.64	2.92	0.72	20.52	
1926	3.80	2.93	0.87	19.64	
1927	4.01	2.86	1.15	18.51	
1928	3.90	2.96	0.94	17.60	
1929	3.86	3.13	0.73	16.93	102.6
1930	4.06	3.32	0.74	16.19	90.0
1931	3.12	3.58	− 0.46	16.80	75.5
1932	1.92	4.66	− 2.74	19.49	57.9
1933	2.00	4.60	− 2.60	22.54	55.5
1934	3.01	6.64	− 3.63	27.05	65.0
1935	3.71	6.50	− 2.79	28.70	72.1
1936	4.00	8.42	− 4.42	33.78	82.4
1937	4.96	7.73	− 2.77	36.42	90.4
1938	5.59	6.76	− 1.17	37.16	84.6
1939	4.98	8.84	− 3.86	40.44	90.5

SOURCE: U.S. Department of Commerce, *Historical Statistics of the United States, Colonial Times to 1970* (Washington, D.C.: Government Printing Office, 1975); and U.S. Department of Commerce, NIPA, 1929–1976 Statistical Tables, September 1981.

The conservative management of the British economy in the 1930s appeared dull or counterproductive to contemporaries. In retrospect, it was probably optimal. Productive activities were adequately funded thanks to the strict fiscal policy followed. Real GDP growth in 1933–1938 compares well with that in any other period in British economic history in the twentieth century. British unemployment in the 1930s was substantially a demographic and institutional phenomenon and cannot be ascribed solely to the Depression.

Governments did not intervene solely through fiscal policy: they enacted numerous regulations. In the United States, the National Industrial

TABLE 2.2   U.K. GOVERNMENT FINANCES
(ADMINISTRATIVE BUDGETS), 1929–1939
CENTRAL GOVERNMENT

	FISCAL YEAR BEGINNING APRIL (IN MILLIONS OF POUNDS STERLING)		
	Receipts	Expenditures	Surplus or deficit (−)
1929	815.0	840.0	− 25.0
1930	857.8	881.0	− 23.2
1931	851.5	859.5	− 8.0
1932	827.0	862.0	− 35.0
1933	809.4	779.2	30.2
1934	804.6	797.1	7.5
1935	844.7	841.8	2.9
1936	896.6	902.2	− 5.6
1937	948.7	919.9	28.8
1938	1,006.2	1,018.9	− 12.7
1939	1,132.2	1,408.2	−276.0

SOURCE: League of Nations Statistical Yearbooks (various issues, 1929–1939).

Recovery Act (NIRA) of June 1933 empowered the president to establish for each industry a code of business practices and set minimum wages, maximum hours, and other conditions of employment. The Sherman Act of 1890, which prohibited monopolies, was suspended with respect to codes that essentially established monopolistic devices. In fact President Roosevelt was following two inconsistent policies. He tried simultaneously to increase prices in order to restore profits and stimulate recovery and to raise wages relative to prices in order to increase consumption: the increases in prices and in wages neutralized each other, and the NIRA led to more problems than to useful results. The Supreme Court ruled the NIRA unconstitutional in May 1935 on the grounds that it improperly delegated powers to the executive branch.

But the NIRA was only one of several attempts to regulate economic activity in order to remedy supposed market failures. The Davis-Bacon Act of 1931 required federal construction projects to pay prevailing wages. The Norris-LaGuardia Act of 1932 established the legality of unionization and collective bargaining. The Agricultural Adjustment Act of 1933 (declared unconstitutional in 1936) established production controls and price supports for farm products. The Banking Act of 1933 established the Federal Deposit Insurance Corporation to insure and regulate banks. The Securities Act of

TABLE 2.3   FRENCH GOVERNMENT FINANCES
(ADMINISTRATIVE BUDGETS), 1929–1939
CENTRAL GOVERNMENT

	CALENDAR YEAR (IN BILLIONS OF FRANCS)			
	Receipts	Expenditures	Surplus or deficit (−)	Deficit as share of expenditures
1929–30[a]	68.3	64.0	4.3	−6.7[b]
1930[c]	50.8	55.7	− 4.9	8.8
1931[c]	47.9	53.4	− 5.5	10.3
1932[d]	36.0	40.7	− 4.7	11.5
1933	43.4	54.9	−11.5	20.9
1934	41.1	49.9	− 8.8	17.6
1935	39.5	49.9	−10.4	20.8
1936	38.9	55.8	−16.9	30.3
1937	44.5	68.2	−23.7	34.8
1938	54.6	82.3	−27.7	33.7
1939	63.7	106.4	−42.7	40.1

SOURCE: Alfred Sauvy, *Histoire économique de la France entre les deux guerres* (Paris: Fayard, 1967).

[a]Fifteen months.

[b]Surplus.

[c]Fiscal year began in April.

[d]Nine months.

1933 regulated public offering of new securities, and the Securities Exchange Act of 1934 established the Securities and Exchange Commission to regulate trading on security exchanges. The Communications Act of 1934 established the Federal Communications Commission to administer communications regulations. The Fishery Cooperative Marketing Act of 1934 exempted cartels of fishermen from antitrust laws. The National Labor Relations Act of 1935 established the National Labor Relations Board to prevent unfair labor practices and required collective bargaining. The Robinson-Patman Act of 1936 amended the Clayton Act to prohibit price discrimination. Not all of these regulations were intrinsically bad, but the incredible aspect of these actions is that they were justified by the belief that the private sector was responsible for the Great Depression.

In Britain also, the government supported monopolistic arrangements in such sectors as coal, cotton, iron and steel, railways, agriculture, and shipbuilding. Markets were protected by quotas, and declining industries were kept less efficient while investment was restricted.

The French government fixed many prices administratively in the period of deflation and subsidized agriculture for obvious political reasons (France was still largely a rural country in the 1930s). When the Popular Front came to power in the second quarter of 1936, Premier Léon Blum drastically cut the workweek while granting large pay increases to all workers: it is estimated that unit labor costs increased by half in the following year. Exports contracted and unemployment rose swiftly. The devaluation of the franc on October 1, 1936, was insufficient, and the franc left the gold standard on June 30, 1937.

The differing actions of France, the United Kingdom, and the United States in the Great Depression constitute almost a controlled laboratory experiment in policymaking.

The United States allowed its financial system to collapse and delivered a mortal blow to the international economy: the largest manufacturing power in the world was almost ruined. When monetary policy permitted the financial system to recover, the economy's progress was rapid although checked by misguided regulatory practices.

The United Kingdom isolated its economy by letting its currency float;[3] then it pursued a moderately expansionary monetary policy in conjunction with a tight fiscal policy. Britain essentially sailed through the deepest (so far) economic contraction in the twentieth century.

France resisted well in the beginning, thanks to the margin of competitiveness left by the undervaluation of the franc in 1928. By refusing to adjust to the devaluation of the dollar in 1933, the French government had to deflate massively in order to reduce the overvaluation of the franc. Large budget deficits resulted from decreasing tax receipts due to falling prices. The private sector had to compete with the government for financing, which was continuously reduced by a decreasing stock of money. The economy stagnated throughout the period.

Monetary policies dominated fiscal policies in the 1930s. Where monetary policies aimed at increasing the liquidity of the economy and sustaining confidence in the banking sector, such as in Britain, a tight fiscal policy assisted economic recovery by permitting an adequate funding of the private sector. Where monetary (including exchange rate) policies were inept, expansionary fiscal policies could not adequately support economic activity while huge public borrowings crowded out the private sector and further weakened the productive sector of the economy. Misguided regulatory practices increased the rigidities of the economic system and generally proved counterproductive.

3

A Theoretical Appraisal of the Great Depression

Both earlier analyses and the wealth of new studies that have appeared in the past twenty years have attributed the Great Depression to one of several causes, including malfunctions in the gold standard, maladjustments in the international economy, and the collapse of expenditures (in one form or another). Many modern attempts to explain the Great Depression also emphasize the importance of the monetary contraction.

In 1929, most of the world currencies were linked by fixed exchange rates on a gold exchange standard. The major difference between the gold exchange standard and the gold standard mechanism was that the former allowed policies designed to insulate countries from the consequences of gold movements. Since at the end of the 1920s, both France and the United States sterilized the influx of gold and other reserves, they stopped the price increases that would have occasioned outflows of gold and restored the equilibrium of the system. This shifted the burden of adjustment to deficit countries. Insofar as this policy contributed to the devaluation of sterling, it deepened the Great Depression, but the gold exchange standard was simply an element leading to one of the causes of the economic crisis under study.

The operation of the gold standard in the 1920s was also affected by the problem of reparations and war debts. Although reparations contributed to the difficulties of Germany, the Depression in Germany started when short-terms funds invested in that country were withdrawn in 1929–1930 and especially 1931 while German export markets were being restricted. The reparations problem could not be more than a source of weakening of German balance of payments.

Much more significant is the explanation based on so-called maladjustments. World War I had caused great changes in economic structures and international trade flows. Two well-balanced economic units, the Austro-

Hungarian empire and Tsarist Russia, had disappeared. New sources of supply of raw materials and manufactures had appeared on all continents. The needed adjustments were partly resisted thanks to large capital exports from the United States, and the maladjustments increased until the international economy collapsed. The only problem with this explanation is that it implicitly assumes an endogenous mechanism by which maladjustments lead to a collapse. The maladjustment explanation cannot be an explanation if it only points to maladjustments. More important, the mechanism was not endogenous but exogenous to the system: the resistance to the "maladjustments" and new sources of supply led to a tariff war that was exogenous to the economic system. It was imposed politically for institutional reasons of overrepresentation of some of the groups that resisted the necessary adjustments. Once the tariff war had started, the international economy (both trade and international lending) faltered in a fragile world of harsh international competition and political difficulties in countries receiving foreign capital. The United States, the most powerful and wealthy nation of the time, was the last country that needed tariff protection in 1930.

Keynesian economists have tried to account for the severity of the Depression by the collapse of one or another category of expenditure; Peter Temin terms these explanations the "spending hypotheses."[1] Temin reviews the spending hypotheses associated with Alvin Hansen, R. A. Gordon, Joseph Schumpeter, Thomas Wilson, and Keynes and the econometric models of the interwar period constructed by Ben Bolch and John Pilgrim, Lawrence Klein, Jan Tinbergen, and John B. Kirkwood. He concludes that all these explanations are unacceptable because they rest on untested assumptions. Temin then offers his own spending hypothesis. According to Temin, the effect on wealth of the stock market crash (through a wealth effect included in a consumption function) cannot account for the autonomous fall in consumption in 1930 since the wealth effect was too small. Temin is partially right on this point. The Dow Jones industrial stock price index fell by 23 percent from 1929 to 1930, but it was still above the average level of 1928. This could certainly have led to a downward adjustment in perceived wealth and actual consumption, but it cannot account for the large reduction in consumption. Temin builds his case by regression analysis on a limited period of time. This leads him to conclude that the actual decline in consumption in 1930 is much larger than the one predicted by his regressions. Thomas Mayer recalculated Temin's equations on a longer period of time and found larger negative residuals in other years of the period.[2] Obviously, Temin needs to explain why a negative residual in 1930 should cause a deep contraction while larger ones did not.[3]

The monetarist variety of explanations are dominated by Milton Friedman and Anna Schwartz. As pointed out before, Friedman and Schwartz, in their classic *Monetary History of the United States*, rightly stress that the one-third reduction in the stock of money from 1929 to 1933 made a large contribution to the Great Depression. But, as we saw earlier, the reduction in the stock of money was not sizable until the first quarter of 1931, while from March 1931 to March 1933, M1 fell by 22 percent and M2 by 30 percent. Hence, the reduction of the stock of money was not the sole cause of the Depression, even though the monetary contraction was the major cause of the Depression before 1931 and especially in 1932–1933.

Robert Gordon and James Wilcox, in explaining the initial phase of the 1929–1933 contraction, do not preclude a role for money in determining the timing of the 1929 turning point but assign the primary role to nonmonetary forces.[4] They also conclude that the Depression was deeper and the recovery slower than can be explained by models relating income to current and past value of money. Allan Meltzer, on behalf of the monetarists, agrees with them on the last point but points out that this certainly does not preclude a major role for money in explaining the Depression.[5]

Gordon and Wilcox assert that the primary nonmonetary source of the 1929–1931 contraction in income was the decline in residential housing construction, due both to a slowing of population growth following the 1921 and 1924 legislation limiting immigration and to overbuilding during the mid-1920s. Since the literature on the Depression often analyzes the housing factor, Meltzer reviews the question carefully. He notes first that the U.S. population growth rate peaked around 1923 and then fell until 1931. During most of the Depression years, the population growth rate rose. Second, the real returns on short-term government securities were between 6 and 13 percent in 1930–1932, and, Meltzer concludes, "the gain from postponing purchases, and lending or purchasing securities instead of borrowing to purchase durables, was high by any historical standard. It does not require an interest elasticity as large as has been found in some recent studies to explain the decline in housing starts after 1929 as mainly a response to demand."[6]

Nominal and real interest rates increased substantially in 1928–1929 while stock market speculation was diverting resources away from housing. It does not appear that the decline in housing in 1929 and in the 1930s was fully autonomous or an independent cause of the Depression; rather it seems that housing starts did not behave atypically in the 1928–1930 business cycle. The value of residential building contracts increased by 8 percent from 1927 to 1928 and was above the levels reached in both 1925 and 1926. It then fell by 31 percent in 1929 and by 42 percent in 1930. Even though the autonomous character of the housing factor in the Depression is not well established, it is obvious that housing contracts were the first to be hit by the restrictive monetary policy of 1928–1929 and played their usual negative role in the downward phase of a business cycle.

There appears to be a consensus emerging from recent work on the Great Depression that both monetary and nonmonetary factors account for the phenomenon under study. But Keynesians still emphasize nonmonetary factors and monetarists, monetary elements. What, then, did happen?

STYLIZED FACTS AND IDENTIFIED CAUSES

The Great Depression in the United States was not one continuous event from 1929 to 1938 but consisted of three distinct episodes:

1. The business cycle period: a cycle from mid-1928 to mid-1930 with economic activity peaking in August 1929;
2. The Depression period: an ever accelerating fall of economic activity from mid-1930 to the first semester of 1933 with economic activity reaching a trough in March 1933;
3. The recovery period: an incomplete recovery until 1937 and a new setback before the war (see Table 3.1).

As mentioned above, the U.S. economy dominated world manufacturing. On average over 1925–1929, U.S. manufacturing production represented 42.5 percent of world manufacturing production. The international transmission of U.S. business cycles was speeded by the general return to fixed exchange rates at the end of the 1920s. But the United States was not immune from foreign influences. The share of exports of goods in the goods-producing sector was 9.4 percent in 1929 (see Table 3.4).

The U.S. farm sector did not suffer a crisis in absolute terms in the 1920s, but it was affected by two relative crises: first, after the exceptionally favorable terms of trade experienced during the war, there was a return to a more normal level of relative prices, comparable to those of the years preceding the war; second, while the GDP of the farm sector increased only slightly through the 1920s, the GDP of the rest of the economy increased at a much faster trend rate of growth. Unfortunately, the farm sector was overrepresented in the U.S. Congress and forced passage of the Hawley-Smoot Tariff in June 1930. The ratio of duties calculated to dutiable imports, which stood on average at 38.9 percent in 1925–1929, jumped to 44.7 percent in 1930, 53.2 percent in 1931, and 59.1 percent in 1932—a 52 percent increase over the average level in the second half of the 1920s.

TABLE 3.1   NATIONAL INCOME AND PRODUCT ACCOUNTS
OF THE UNITED STATES, 1929–1939
(IN BILLIONS OF 1972 DOLLARS)

					INDEXES[e]	
	GDP^a	G^b	X^c	I^d	GDP	$G + X$
1929	313.2	41.0	16.7	55.8	100.0	100.0
1930	283.3	44.8	14.2	38.6	90.5	102.3
1931	261.6	46.3	11.7	23.7	83.5	100.5
1932	225.6	44.3	9.3	7.9	72.0	92.9
1933	220.9	42.9	9.1	8.4	70.5	90.1
1934	238.0	48.4	9.7	13.0	76.0	100.7
1935	258.7	49.6	10.5	24.0	82.6	104.1
1936	294.5	57.9	11.2	32.2	94.0	119.8
1937	308.7	55.8	14.0	39.7	98.6	121.0
1938	295.1	60.7	13.5	24.0	94.2	128.6
1939	318.2	63.0	14.3	33.6	101.6	134.0

SOURCE: U.S. Department of Commerce, NIPA, September 1981.
NOTE: GDP figures differ from those in Table 1.1; see Table 1.1.
[a]In real terms.
[b]Government purchases of goods and services in real terms.
[c]Exports of goods and services in real terms.
[d]Gross private domestic investment in real terms.
[e]1929 = 100.

After the failure of the Austrian Creditanstalt in May 1931, large withdrawals of short-term credits forced Germany to default successively on its governmental and private obligations to foreigners. This led to the devaluation of the British pound in September 1931.

The U.S. stock of money (both M1 and M2) went almost unchanged from January 1928 to April 1930 and fell marginally until March 1931. Then, from March 1931 to March 1933, M1 fell by 22 percent and M2 by 30 percent.

Started by the U.S. Hawley-Smoot Tariff of June 1930 and exacerbated by the British devaluation of September 1931 and the British Abnormal Importations Act of November 1931, the trade war raged in the 1930s in two directions: first, trade became bilateral or regional within existing empires; second, tariff restrictions were increasingly complemented by administrative measures, such as prohibitions, quotas, licensing systems, and clearing agreements. In value terms, international trade fell by 60 percent from 1929 to 1932 and remained below the 1932 level until 1937. By 1933 the interna-

TABLE 3.2   NATIONAL INCOME AND PRODUCT ACCOUNTS
OF THE UNITED KINGDOM, 1929–1938
(IN MILLIONS OF POUNDS; IN CONSTANT 1938 PRICES)

| | GDP^a | G^b | X^c | I^d | INDEXES[e] | |
					GDP	$G + X$
1929	4,726	444	986	461	100.0	100.0
1930	4,720	455	849	463	99.9	91.2
1931	4,480	466	684	454	94.8	80.4
1932	4,493	466	669	396	95.1	79.4
1933	4,544	471	678	409	96.1	80.3
1934	4,851	482	704	498	102.6	82.9
1935	5,033	515	794	518	106.5	91.5
1936	5,190	562	771	565	109.8	93.2
1937	5,411	627	810	584	114.5	100.5
1938	5,572	749	757	592	117.9	105.3

SOURCE: C. H. Feinstein, *National Income, Expenditure, and Output of the United Kingdom, 1855–1965* (Cambridge, Eng.: Cambridge University Press, 1972).
[a]In real terms.
[b]Public authorities' current expenditure on goods and services in real terms.
[c]Exports of goods and services in real terms.
[d]Gross domestic fixed capital formation in real terms.
[e]1929 = 100.

tional economy had collapsed. It was not to recover until after World War II.

To understand the world depression, we must first understand the U.S. depression.

The main cause of the end of the upward phase of the 1928–1930 business cycle was undoubtedly the tight monetary policy followed after the beginning of 1929: the real stock of money was essentially constant in 1928–1929, interest rates rose, and the housing sector collapsed in 1929. After the middle of 1929, industrial production, profits, and the stock exchange returned to their 1928 level.

The two main causes of the Depression are the collapse of the international economy and the collapse of the U.S. financial system. All the major powers contributed to the collapse of the international economy; an act of the U.S. government (due to institutional factors) that was exogenous to and resisted by the core of the economy initiated the trade war. The collapse of the international economy increased business uncertainty, greatly re-

TABLE 3.3　NATIONAL INCOME AND PRODUCT ACCOUNTS
OF FRANCE, 1929–1938
(IN BILLIONS OF FRANCS;
IN CONSTANT AVERAGE PRICES OF 1901–1910)

	GDP^a	G^b	X^c	I^d	$G + X^e$
1929	100	9.4	9.2	11.7	100.0
1930	97	11.3	8.3	13.0	105.4
1931	93	11.3	7.1	11.5	98.9
1932	89	12.2	5.4	9.4	94.6
1933	93	12.7	5.5	9.3	97.8
1934	93	12.2	5.7	8.7	96.2
1935	90	13.0	5.2	8.5	97.8
1936	91	13.4	4.9	8.9	98.4
1937	96	14.3	5.3	9.6	105.4
1938	96	13.6	5.8	8.7	104.3

SOURCE: Jean-Jacques Carré, Paul Dubois, and Edmond Malinvaud, *La Croissance française* (Paris: Seuil, 1972).
[a]Index in real terms.
[b]Government purchases of goods and services in real terms.
[c]Exports of goods and services in real terms.
[d]Gross private domestic investment in real terms.
[e]Index 1929 = 100.

stricted the markets of the internationally traded–goods sector of the economies of the United States and its trading partners (see Table 3.4), and finally exacerbated the difficulties of the U.S. financial system.

During the banking crisis at the end of 1930 and from March 1931 on, the American public converted deposits into currency, and banks strengthened their reserve position by liquidating available assets. The U.S. monetary authorities did not respond to what was a large financial disintermediation movement in a sophisticated economy that could not function without an orderly system of payments. The devaluation of sterling in September 1931 worsened the uncertainty, and the monetary authorities further jolted the system by sizably increasing the discount rate. When they failed to check a renewed reduction in the stock of money in 1932, business confidence plummeted and financial disintermediation accelerated. The U.S. banking system crashed in the first quarter of 1933 and closed down in March 1933.

The two main causes of the incomplete recovery were the continued disorganization of the international economy and misguided government

TABLE 3.4   SHARE OF EXPORTS OF GOODS IN
GOODS-PRODUCING SECTOR, 1929–1938
(PERCENTAGES)

	United States	United Kingdom	Germany	France
1929	9.4	34.1	21.6	19.5
1930	8.3	27.6	21.8	16.8
1931	6.7	20.9	20.7	12.6
1932	6.3	19.7	15.6	9.1
1933	6.3	19.4	12.8	8.8
1934	6.4	20.2	9.5	9.5
1935	6.0	20.4	8.7	8.4
1936	5.7	18.0	8.7	7.4
1937	6.8	22.1	9.6	9.5
1938	7.1	19.7	7.7	9.9

NOTE: Since the breakdown of GNP by major type of product is available for the United States (Source: U.S. Department of Commerce, NIPA, September 1981), the numbers for the United States are computed directly. I noticed in a 1945 League of Nations publication (*Industrialization and Foreign Trade*) that the distribution of the gainfully employed population in the United States in 1930 between agriculture-mining-marketing and the rest is a good indication of the distribution of output among the various sectors. I assumed the same was true for the other countries and multiplied the shares of exports in GNP in Table 1.14 by the following coefficients to get Table 3.2: United Kingdom, 2.4; Germany, 1.5; France, 1.4.

policies that reduced the efficiency and the potency of the self-correcting mechanism of the private economy once the financial system started to function again.

But how did these causes lead to the consequences observed?

THE COMPETING MODELS

Economic theory is the study of the determinants of allocation and optimal decisionmaking to allocate the scarce resources of a society to serve competing demands; economic history is the study of the determinants of the actual allocation of scarce resources in a given society. Depending on the location of the society in time and space, the scarce resources will differ (water or fresh air might be more or less plentiful). In modern industrial societies, the scarce resources that receive the most analytical attention are capital and labor. The growth of a society's wealth depends in large part on optimally combining the existing amounts or stocks of capital and labor. In this context, nothing is more frustrating to a society and its scholars than the existence at a given moment in time or for long periods of time of unused or underutilized scarce resources such as excess productive capacity or unemployment of labor.

Through time, a price system has evolved to express the value of scarce resources in a common standard, which could be any commodity and was gold for many centuries. Gold, later notes, and more generally money are units of account and media of exchange. Money is also a store of value. Money buys goods, but goods do not buy money.[7] This leads many to wonder whether money, in a monetary economy, is just a "veil" with no effect on real activity or whether changes in the quantity of money do affect real activity. This question is at the core of the theoretical debate in macroeconomics and monetary economics.

The quantity of money (M) multiplied by the speed or velocity (V) at which it circulates represents the total nominal amount of transactions in a given period of time, which can be approximated by the nominal value of output or equivalently by output (Y) times the price level (P). Then MV equals PY. In other words the aggregate supply of commodities (PY) equals aggregate demand (MV). When the output of a society is at such a level that there are no unused resources, it is called either the full employment level of output or the potential level of output (Y^*). The existing stock of real money balances (M/P) in a given period of time is related to real activity according to the equation $M/P = Y/V$. In a monetary economy, real activity thus depends not only on the stocks of capital or labor to determine the optimal or potential output, but on the ratio between the stock of real money balances and output (that is, the reciprocal of V) that the economic agents in a given society can maintain due to institutional factors and wish to maintain due to their perception of the economic environment.

If the economic agents who allocate scarce resources between their uses in space and over time knew the prices (and hence the relative scarcities) of all goods in space and over time, all decisions of individual agents (whether households, firms, or government) would be permanently reconciled. The economy would be in state of continuous equilibrium. But few markets for future goods exist, and hence decisions are made in a world of uncertainty (conversely because of uncertainty, few markets for future goods exist). Furthermore when existing prices change rapidly, it is hard to distinguish between movements in absolute and in relative prices. In spite of these drawbacks, the neoclassical school of economic thinking assumes that the optimal allocation of the scarce resources at the disposal of society is best performed through the price system. Deviations of actual from expected prices largely explain the differences or gap between actual and full employment output, but economic agents carry out all mutually perceived advantageous exchanges, and in this sense, the economy is in equilibrium. For the neoclassical school, relative prices must reflect relative scarcities, and hence prices must be flexible.

The monetarists who belong to the neoclassical school further assume that the demand for money is a stable behavioral relationship; this leads them to advocate constant growth in the money supply in order to promote the stability of the economic system.

The neo-Keynesian school assumes that prices are not fully flexible and that they do not adjust rapidly enough to clear markets. Consequently, economic agents face quantity constraints—they are constrained by levels of sales or employment different from those they would voluntarily choose to demand or supply at prevailing wages and prices. This can lead to a permanent state of underemployment of an economy's scarce resources. It will then be necessary to increase the level of aggregate demand in the economy, which is equal to the sum of consumption (C), investment (I), government expenditure (G), and net exports (exports $[X]$ minus imports). If consumption is assumed to be related in a stable fashion to disposable income, it can be shown that the level of output will be determined by fixed multipliers applied to so-called autonomous expenditures such as I, G, or X. This algebra of multipliers is justified only if the price level is stable.

The rational expectations school recognizes that information on all prices is not available;[8] on the other hand, current prices, by reflecting current and expected demand and supply, are set given expectations about future prices. As Robert E. Lucas notes, "One needs a principle to reconcile the price distributions implied by the market equilibrium with the distributions used by agents to form their own views of the future."[9] Twenty years ago, John Muth noted that the general principle of the absence of economic rents in competitive equilibrium implied that these distributions could not differ systematically. His term for this latter hypothesis was "rational expectations."[10] The rational expectations hypothesis allows us to build equilibrium models of the business cycle that do not rely on the concepts of excess demand and supply. Instead, unforeseen shocks to the economy and partial information lead to deviations of actual from expected prices that will, as does the neoclassical or monetarist analysis, largely explain the gap between actual and full employment output.

To summarize, prices play a crucial role in allocating the scarce resources of a monetary economy. Expected prices (or their distributions) for future goods are reflected in current prices so that decisionmaking in a state of uncertainty can be carried out rationally. Still, due to unforeseen shocks or partial information, actual prices will differ from expected prices. If one assumes that prices are flexible, all exchanges perceived as mutually advantageous will be carried out, and the economy, in this sense, will be in equilibrium. Otherwise, the economy would be in disequilibrium, and state intervention along neo-Keynesian channels would be required to restore full employment.

Modern versions of neo-Keynesian or monetarist analysis using the rational expectations hypothesis conclude that a shock to aggregate nominal demand, whether originating in an unexpected change in the quantity of money or not, affects the real activity of the economy by creating discrepancies between expected and actual price changes. And state intervention is justified or not, according to whether prices are assumed to be rigid or flexible.

Since changes in the quantity of money and in aggregate demand are closely related, the channel by which changes in the quantity of money affect real activity is identified, as long as one can show that changes in the quantity of money "cause" the changes in aggregate demand. The question of causality between changes in the quantity of money and national income has long been the subject of controversy. But the overall econometric evidence seems to suggest that money changes affect income changes more than the reverse.

Again, economic agents (households, firms, governments) make decisions in a state of uncertainty. This uncertainty is general for decisions concerning the future since they depend on the realization of expected events and partial for decisions concerning the present due to limited information regarding relevant phenomena. Economic agents can alleviate this uncertainty by observing recurrent phenomena in a society operating within a stable institutional framework. But if mild or *a fortiori* violent shocks (such as the collapse of the economy's financial system) that disturb the structure and organization of the economy or alterations in the institutional framework deprive economic agents of the benefit of such observations in predicting the future, not only will deviations of expected from actual prices very likely be larger than usual, but, and more important, economic agents will divert larger and larger amounts of scarce resources from productive to protective investments. They will carry out mutually perceived advantageous exchanges, but large amounts of resources will appear to be idle when in fact economic agents are keeping them in reserve in order to face the increased level of uncertainty. Consequently, for a given level of activity in a world of stable or declining prices but with a sudden increase in uncertainty, economic agents might demand a larger amount of real money balances (money balances in real terms) while producers might reduce stocks of goods maintained to serve expected future demand if they expect the level or growth of that demand to fall.

Thus, for a given level of economic activity of a society (even one relatively independent from the rest of the world), a sudden change in perceived uncertainty (in a period of stable or declining prices) due, for example, to the collapse of the international economy in which the society operates will lead to *ex ante* changes in the demand for real money balances and the level of stocks. If the authorities do not accommodate this increased demand for real money balances, the private sector will permanently adjust the level of real activity (or prices will fall) in order to attain the desired ratio between real output and the existing stock of real money balances. Activity will be temporarily further adjusted to reduce stocks of goods to desired levels. *Ex post*, the system will be in equilibrium with the desired ratios between activity and its determinants.

There is a distinction here between primary and proximate causes. The change in the level of uncertainty is the primary cause of future changes in the economy, while the nonaccommodation of the increased demand for real money balances is the proximate cause or channel by which future changes are effected. In this sense, if the original shock is indeed the primary cause of future changes, the proximate cause is the only channel through which actual changes in the economy are brought about. By being the proximate cause of changes in the above example, the monetary authorities bear the full responsibility for those changes. Further, if the public *ex ante* demand for an increased level of real money balances held in the form of currency leads to a financial disintermediation that is not remedied by the monetary authorities, they again bear full responsibility for the reduction in the stock of money or the eventual collapse of the financial system. As the private sector desperately tries to achieve an ever higher ratio of real money balances to activity as the uncertainty increases (in a period of stable or declining prices), a cumulative process of increased uncertainty leading to *ex ante* increased demand for money and to an *ex post* adjustment of the real activity will sharply curtail output in the wake of the reduction in the stock of money.

Technically, I am asserting that the demand for real money balances depends critically on expectations of the future evolution of the environment in which an economy operates. The demand for real money balances is stable, given a stable institutional and structural environment. But at times of sudden changes in the economic or institutional structure, the demand for real money balances shifts. At a given level of real activity (in a period of stable or declining prices), the *ex ante* short-term demand for real money balances will likely increase in the transition period from one steady state of the economy to the next; the *ex ante* long-term demand for real money balances will increase if the change of steady states is perceived to be less conducive, and decrease if the change is perceived to be more conducive, to the optimal allocation of scarce resources in order to satisfy the needs of society (for a given level of uncertainty, the *ex ante* demand for real money balances will increase if activity increases and vice versa).[11] One should not mistake, in this context, changes in political regimes, say, as having more than temporary effects on the *ex ante* demand for money as long as the basic allocative system of scarce resources is perceived to be maintained. It is not contradictory, for example, that the demand for real money balances can be econometrically estimated to be stable over a century of Italian history, while it shifted in the United States when the financial system collapsed.

Since institutional reforms can modify the relationship between output and employment, changes in employment do not necessarily equate with changes in output. In other words, a given increase in production cannot reduce a given level of unemployment if institutional reforms change the determinants of the labor supply. Hence an increase in unemployment benefits might reduce the expected increase in employment associated with a given increase in output, which will then be due to such factors as increases in productivity or in the number of hours worked by those who have a job.

How does this framework explain the channels by which the causes identified in the preceding section led to the Depression?

THE MECHANISM OF THE DEPRESSION

In the upward phase of the business cycle from mid-1928 to mid-1929, uncertainty was decreasing due to rising business activity, and the ratio of real money balances to output was falling. But there are obvious limits to the increase in the velocity of money (for a given organization of the financial system, the stock of money can finance only so many transactions). When economic agents realized in the fall of 1929 that the economy had stopped growing in the middle of the year, perceived uncertainty returned to more normal levels, and the *ex ante* demand for real money balances increased. Real activity adjusted to prevailing conditions and desired ratios between activity and its determinants. From mid-1928 to almost mid-1930, the U.S. economy experienced a rather typical business cycle. But the environment of the economy began to be modified when discussions for a tariff increase started seriously in the winter of 1929 and culminated in the signing of the Hawley-Smoot Tariff on June 17, 1930, to the dismay of the business community. Six weeks earlier, more than a thousand economists had written: "There are already many evidences that such action would inevitably provoke other countries to pay us back in kind by levying retaliatory duties against our goods."[12] The perceived level of uncertainty cannot but have increased further and further throughout 1931 and 1932 as other countries did pay the United States back in kind. The *ex ante* increased demand for real money balances was not met, and financial disintermediation began (the demand for real money balances was increased as well because of the desire to hold money at a time of falling prices).

Furthermore, due to the actual impact of reduced exports on the output of the internationally traded–goods sector, the collapse of the international economy directly affected the level of real activity in the United States. Uncertainty created by the failure of world-famous financial institutions peaked when sterling left the gold standard in September 1931. Britain was the financial center of the world, and the devaluation of its currency could not but have worried economic agents around the world. The Federal Reserve had to increase the U.S. discount rate considerably to stem capital exports. The *ex ante* demand for real money balances increased further and still was not met. Financial disintermediation reached unprecedented levels, and aggregate demand was dramatically cut. The combination of the multiplier effect of reduced exports and the decreasing stock of money, which was leading to a continuous downward adjustment of economic activity to re-establish the desired ratio of real money balances to output, caused a collapse of production. While aggregate demand was being reduced, prices fell but never enough to give the desired amount of real money balances. The financial system finally collapsed, bringing the economy to a standstill.

The collapse of the international economy, the increased level of uncertainty, and the financial disintermediation that followed were the primary causes (through the reduction in the stock of money) of the fall in activity. Monetary policy and the reduction in the stock of money, particularly the refusal or the failure to accommodate the *ex ante* increase in the demand for real money balances, were the main proximate causes of the Great Depression. The reduction in exports was the other proximate cause of the reduction of output.

The above framework also explains the limited recovery. The increase in the real quantity of money in 1934–1936 finally satisfied the demand for real money balances, and output started to increase. But due to the continued disorganization of the international economy, the desired ratio of real money balances to output was much higher than before 1930, and an econometric regression fitted over the interwar period will lead to the false conclusion that the link between money and nominal income had weakened after 1933; rather the nature of the link was modified. Furthermore, institutional changes of considerable magnitude modified the structure of the economy and contributed to maintaining at very high levels the perceived uncertainty and the *ex ante* demand for real money balances. The large increase in the real quantity of money satisfied an increasing demand due to the recovery (the need for transaction balances) at a time when the level of uncertainty remained high; the cause of the uncertainty had changed from the collapse of the financial system to misguided institutional reforms while the international economy remained disorganized, but the level of uncertainty never fell to its pre-1930 level, even though it was reduced compared with the 1931–1933 level.

The case of Great Britain confirms this analysis. The increase in uncertainty also increased the *ex ante* demand for real money balances, especially during the collapse of the U.S. financial system in 1932–1933, but the devaluation of sterling in 1931 gave the British economy a margin of security and limited the reduction in exports. There was no financial disintermediation since the banking system retained the confidence of the public. After the reorientation of the British production system from the export to the domestic market, which was helped by adequate financing, the supply of real money balances was sufficient to foster a remarkable recovery of output even though unemployment remained high.

The Depression in the United States resulted from a combination of the multiplier effect of the fall in exports and the reduction in the stock of money at a time of increased *ex ante* demand for real money balances as well as various distributional factors. In the case of France, these distributional factors played a large role. Increased budget deficits financed by savings in 1933–1936 crowded the private economy out of the financial markets, aborting several recoveries. Furthermore, the Depression especially hit the traded-goods sector of the international economy, which is usually the most efficient at combining scarce resources to satisfy the needs of society.

As the literature on the subject increasingly recognizes, the Great Depression cannot be explained by a single cause, monetary or nonmonetary. But most of the primary causes would not have contributed to the crisis as much as they did if the United States had adopted a strong countercyclical monetary policy and if sterling had not been devalued in September 1931 beyond what was required. Above all, if the United States had not started a trade war in June 1930, the world economy might not have collapsed.

CONCLUSIONS

The previous analysis might underestimate, in the view of some readers, the impact of domestic nonmonetary causes (such as reductions in consumption on investment due to changes in institutions, expectations, fiscal policy, demography) and the trade war, and they may feel that more attention should be given to autonomous spending. This is done in Tables 3.1–3.3. Government spending (G) and exports (X) are generally accepted as largely determined exogenously (by fiscal policy and the demand in the rest of the world). The level of autonomous spending (*G* plus *X*) did not change from 1929 to 1931 in the United States. From 1931 to 1933, GDP fell by 16 percent and autonomous spending by 10 percent. Since the financial system collapsed in 1932–1933, the reduction of *G* plus *X* is not fully autonomous in that period. Nevertheless the reduction in autonomous spending obviously did not help and accounted for part of the reduction in output in 1932–1933.

The British situation is very interesting in this context. The sum of *G* and *X* fell considerably in 1930–1931, and output was reduced; but autonomous spending did not recover in 1932–1934, although output was increasing substantially: the counteracting power of monetary policy is nowhere more obvious than in Britain.

In France, autonomous spending recovered marginally in 1933 and was stable through 1936, while the stock of money was slightly decreasing. Neither the evolution of autonomous spending nor that of the money supply helped the productive sector.

Thus, the evolution of autonomous spending in the 1930s does not appear to have had a strong impact on the crisis. A Keynesian would argue that investment belongs to autonomous demand and contend that investment spending caused the variations in activity. To prove this, one would need to show that movements in investment spending preceded movements in real activity. This is not the case in the United Kingdom, where activity fell in 1931 and investment fell in 1932 (see Table 3.2). In France, in 1930, the movements were converse, with investment increasing while activity fell. In the United States, movements in investment and activity were contemporaneous.

The evolution of nonresidential investment (see Table 3.5) and changes in business inventories could fit an explanation relying on the accelerator, with investment responding with greater variability to previous movements in real activity. But the increase in uncertainty in 1930–1932 could have shifted the investment schedule and reduced the quantity of investment for a given rate of interest, while the real interest rate was increasing sharply (due to falling prices); a multiplier effect of the negative change in investment would obviously have reduced output.

An expansionary monetary policy, by lowering the real rate of interest and increasing activity, would have countered the investment slump. It is therefore difficult to assign responsibilities for the reduction in investment between the effects of monetary policy (increase in real rate of interest and decrease in overall activity) and nonmonetary causes in the United States.

One should obviously distinguish at this point between what caused the Depression and how it was propagated. It is clear that a fall in investment (whatever the causes) will hurt real activity. One could suggest an increase in government spending to counter the investment slump. But then the

TABLE 3.5   COMPONENTS OF U.S. GROSS PRIVATE
DOMESTIC INVESTMENT, 1929–1936
(IN BILLIONS OF 1972 DOLLARS)

	I *(total)*	Nonresi- dential *investment*	*Residential*	Change in business *inventories*
1929	55.8	37.5	13.7	4.6
1930	38.6	30.9	8.2	−0.5
1931	23.7	19.8	6.9	−3.0
1932	7.9	11.5	3.6	−7.2
1933	8.4	10.4	2.8	−4.9
1934	13.0	12.5	3.9	−3.3
1935	24.0	15.6	5.5	2.9
1936	32.2	21.4	7.0	3.8

SOURCE: U.S. Department of Commerce, NIPA, September 1981.

question becomes If monetary policy is the cause, why not deal with it directly instead of replacing one problem with another (how will the government deficit be financed and what if excessive government borrowing crowds the private sector out of financial markets)?

The Great Depression was caused not by one factor, but by several. Nonmonetary causes (other than exports) played a not unnegligible role, but the collapse of the international economy directly or indirectly and the decline in the stock of money were the principal causes of the deepest contraction in economic activity in this century—so far. Great Britain essentially escaped the Depression by a combination of expansionary monetary policy and tight fiscal policy at a time of falling prices. In an inflationary world, this policy mix would not necessarily be optimal. But the counter-cyclical role of monetary policy is nevertheless established by the various policy experiences of the Great Depression. On the other hand, movements in autonomous spending do not seem to account for a very large part of the variations in economic activity.

The case of Sweden in the 1930s confirms the countercyclical effectiveness of monetary policy. As Sweden left the gold standard in September 1931, the authorities declared that the aim of the policy of the Riksbank (the Swedish central bank) should be to "preserve the domestic purchasing power of the *krona* using all available means." According to Swedish economist Lars Jonung, this is the first time that price stability was made the official goal of a central bank. The money stock was kept constant through various measures; first, Sweden left the gold standard and depreciated the krona in 1931; second, the Riksbank supported and lent liberally to the commercial banking system; and third, large purchases of foreign assets from the Swedish public represented a form of expansionary open-market operations. "The monetary program of 1931 and the subsequent declarations of the government and Parliament about the aim of monetary policy maintained public trust and confidence in the banking system."[13] The policy proved very effective. Prices were stable from 1931 to 1936 while output, after the shock of reduced exports, started to increase again in 1933 and surpassed 1929 levels as early as 1934.

This confirms, if confirmation is needed, that governments can start depressions through misguided monetary, regulatory, or tariff policies; it also shows that governments can limit the extent of nominal or real shocks on the economic system by pursuing a monetary policy whose main role is to maintain the stock of money on a stable growth path while accommodating changes in the quantity of money demanded when the economic environment is drastically altered.

Can these lessons be useful for the 1980s?

PART II

THE GREAT STAGNATION

NOTE: Data for 1983 and 1984 are estimates and forecasts. The cutoff date for information used in the compilation of the forecasts in the IMF's *World Economic Outlook* (1983) was April 1983; that of the OECD's *Economic Outlook* (December 1983) was November 21, 1983.

4

The Evolution and Causes of the Modern Economic Crisis

This chapter reviews, from a historical perspective, the main aspects of the international economy in the early 1980s. Part I told the story of a past crisis. The present crisis is still unfolding. It is much more difficult, in this instance, to determine and emphasize the driving forces at work, and the style, from narrative, necessarily becomes speculative.

ECONOMIC CYCLES, 1960–1983

Some definitions are necessary for the international comparisons of national products that follow.

The Organization for Economic Cooperation and Development (OECD) was instituted, by an agreement that became effective on September 30, 1961, in order to foster international cooperation in economic decisionmaking.[1] Its 24 members are industrialized countries: the United States, Canada, Japan, the ten members of the European Economic Community (EEC: Germany, France, United Kingdom, Italy, Belgium, the Netherlands, Luxembourg, Ireland, Denmark, and Greece), Iceland, Norway, Sweden, Finland, Switzerland, Austria, Spain, Portugal, Turkey, Australia, and New Zealand.

The International Monetary Fund (IMF) was instituted by an international monetary conference held at Bretton Woods, New Hampshire, in 1944, to help administer the international monetary system. As of March 15, 1983, the IMF had 146 member-countries (including all members of the OECD except Switzerland), essentially all the countries of the world except the Soviet Union and some of its allies.

In what follows, the "21 industrialized countries" refers to the members of the OECD minus Portugal, Greece, and Turkey, and the group of the "seven major industrial countries" consists of the United States, Japan, Germany, France, United Kingdom, Italy, and Canada.

The "oil-exporting developing countries" (those countries whose oil exports—net of any imports of crude oil—account for at least two-thirds of the country's total exports and are at least 100 million barrels a year) are Algeria, Indonesia, Iran, Iraq, Kuwait, Libya, Nigeria, Oman, Qatar, Saudi Arabia, the United Arab Emirates, and Venezuela.

The other developing countries, or "non-oil developing countries," essentially include all IMF members except those listed above as being industrial countries or oil-exporting developing countries.

Among the non-oil developing countries, mention will be made of the "major exporters of manufactures"—Argentina, Brazil, Greece, Hong Kong, Israel, Korea, Portugal, Singapore, South Africa, and Yugoslavia.

All averages for the respective groups in the tables below are weighted averages with weights proportionate to the U.S. dollar values of the respective GNPs (or GDPs in some cases).

International Comparisons of National Products

International comparisons of national products based on purchasing power parities (PPP) are prepared by the OECD and given below.[2] Table 4.1 presents GDP in current dollars using PPP, and Table 4.2 gives the share of some countries and the EEC in the total GDP of the OECD.

A few conclusions emerge from these tables. First, there was very little relative decline in U.S. economic power in the 1970s. The share of the United States in the GDP of the OECD was six points above the share of the EEC in 1981, as it was in 1970. The progress of Japan in the 1970s was notable but much less spectacular than reported in the media. Above all, the national output of the United States was larger than the combined output of Japan, Germany, France, and the United Kingdom in 1970; it still was in 1981.

Second, Japan has replaced the United Kingdom as the second largest industrial country in the 1970s as compared with 1925–1929 (Germany was the second largest industrial country then, but the financial strength of the United Kingdom gave it the second spot in 1925–1929 behind the United States).

Third, the United States still dominates the noncommunist world economy at the beginning of the 1980s, as it did in the 1970s and the late 1920s. It bears the responsibilities of a world economic leader. Japan is next.

TABLE 4.1   GDP IN CURRENT DOLLARS USING PPP, 1970–1981
(IN BILLIONS OF U.S. DOLLARS)

	United States	Japan	Germany	France	United Kingdom	EEC
1970	988.7	316.4	222.9	174.7	182.2	854.6
1971	1,073.2	348.6	242.6	194.1	197.2	931.5
1972	1,180.0	395.7	263.8	214.6	210.4	1,012.0
1973	1,315.3	454.8	291.0	238.7	238.8	1,131.8
1974	1,420.9	489.4	318.5	267.9	257.0	1,251.7
1975	1,538.8	546.2	342.2	292.9	278.5	1,349.1
1976	1,705.9	608.0	381.2	325.0	305.1	1,498.3
1977	1,903.1	678.3	416.9	355.3	327.6	1,626.7
1978	2,140.4	765.5	462.3	394.9	365.3	1,806.0
1979	2,382.2	875.1	523.3	443.4	403.7	2,029.8
1980	2,599.0	999.2	583.3	491.5	433.0	2,249.2
1981	2,906.3	1,126.7	639.0	538.6	463.9	2,448.1

SOURCE: OECD, *National Accounts, 1952–1981*, vol. 1 (Paris, 1983).

TABLE 4.2   SHARE IN OECD TOTALS: GDP IN CURRENT DOLLARS
USING PPP, 1970–1981
(IN PERCENTAGES)

	United States	Japan	Germany	France	United Kingdom	EEC
1970	38.8	12.4	8.8	6.9	7.2	33.5
1971	38.6	12.5	8.7	7.0	7.1	33.5
1972	38.5	12.9	8.6	7.0	6.9	33.1
1973	38.3	13.2	8.5	7.0	7.0	33.0
1974	37.7	13.0	8.5	7.1	6.8	33.3
1975	37.5	13.3	8.4	7.1	6.8	32.9
1976	37.6	13.4	8.4	7.2	6.7	33.0
1977	38.1	13.6	8.3	7.1	6.6	32.5
1978	38.3	13.7	8.3	7.1	6.5	32.3
1979	38.0	14.0	8.4	7.1	6.5	32.4
1980	37.5	14.4	8.4	7.1	6.3	32.5
1981	37.8	14.6	8.3	7.0	6.0	31.8

SOURCE: OECD, *National Accounts, 1952–1981*, vol. 1 (Paris, 1983).

International Economic Cycles in the 1960s and 1970s[3]

The break in economic growth in 1974 is generally associated with the oil crisis. The GDP of the OECD (and of the EEC) increased at an average annual rate of about 5 percent from 1961 to 1973 and 2.5 percent from 1974 to 1980. U.S. real growth was slightly slower than the OECD average before 1973 and was at the average level from 1974 to 1980.

A slowdown in productivity increases accounts for a large share of the reduction in real growth. The average annual rate of growth of productivity for the OECD economies fell from 3.8 percent in 1968–1973 to 1.5 percent in 1974–1980. It is crucial to understand why increases in productivity were so reduced in 1974–1980 compared with the previous period. The supply of labor was abundant, but the growth rate of investment collapsed. The average annual rate of increase of real gross fixed capital formation (or investment) in the OECD plummeted from 6 percent in 1968–1973 to 0.6 percent in 1974–1980; more important with respect to productivity, the rate of growth of investment in machinery and equipment in the OECD fell from 7.3 percent in 1968–1973 to 2.3 percent in 1974–1980. It is tempting to associate the reduction in investment with the change in relative prices between energy and other goods and services following the oil shock, which made obsolete part of the accumulated technological knowledge acquired while energy was cheap; finding and implementing new technologies in a world of expensive energy is a time-consuming process. Also, uncertainty about demand for goods and services after the oil shock has reduced the desired level of investment for given costs.

The change in the distribution of national income might provide a further explanation for the reduction in investment. Domestic factor incomes are divided between the operating surplus[4] and the compensation of employees.[5] Table 4.3 gives the share of employee compensation in domestic factor incomes for the United States, EEC, and OECD.

The share of compensation was essentially stable in the United States and OECD from 1960 to 1968 and from 1963 to 1968 in the EEC. It then increased substantially in all three areas from 1969 to 1974. Thereafter, it stabilized at or below the 1974 level in the United States but increased further in the EEC and OECD. The general reduction in the share of the operating surplus could have entailed a decrease in the incentive to invest in 1969–1974 that was revealed by the oil shock: as long as the economy was growing, investment was proceeding; when uncertainty increased as the recession occurred, there was no incentive to solve, by an increase in investment, the problems associated with the new environment of expensive energy.

TABLE 4.3   SHARE OF THE COMPENSATION OF EMPLOYEES
IN DOMESTIC FACTOR INCOMES
(PERCENTAGES)

	United States	*EEC*	*OECD*
1960	72.4	61.5	66.8
1961	72.3	62.8	67.0
1962	71.8	63.7	67.0
1963	71.5	64.5	67.1
1964	71.5	64.7	67.1
1965	70.6	64.9	66.9
1966	71.2	65.5	67.5
1967	72.4	65.2	67.9
1968	73.3	64.5	68.0
1969	75.0	64.9	68.8
1970	77.3	66.4	70.2
1971	76.7	67.5	70.7
1972	76.4	67.4	70.2
1973	76.1	67.9	69.8
1974	78.2	70.3	71.9
1975	77.6	72.3	72.9
1976	77.5	71.6	72.8
1977	76.9	71.5	72.8
1978	77.1	71.4	72.3
1979	77.6	71.5	72.2
1980	78.5	72.8	73.3

SOURCE: OECD, *National Accounts, 1951–1980*, vol. 1 (Paris, 1982).

U.S. Economic Cycles, 1977–1982

Inflation in the United States, which reached an annual average of 8 percent in 1974–1980 (compared with 10 percent in the OECD), had to be brought under control, and the United States tightened its monetary policy in the fall of 1979. M1 in the United States (end-of-period stocks), which grew at an average annual rate of 8 percent in 1977–1979, increased by 7.3 percent in 1980, 5.0 percent in 1981, and 8.5 percent in 1982. The annual rate of growth of M2 increased from an average of 9 percent in 1977–1980 to 9.3 percent in 1981–1982. Measured by real interest rates, monetary policy became increasingly restrictive. U.S. real short-term interest rates, which were negative until 1978, increased from below 2 percent in 1979–1980 to above 4 percent in 1981–1982. Real long-term rates shot up from less than 1 percent in 1979 to almost 7 percent in 1982.

At first, inflation as measured by the GNP deflator went almost unchanged from 1980 to 1981, but after more than two years of tight monetary policy and on the expectation that the Federal Reserve would pursue a policy of monetary restraint, inflation finally started to abate in 1982. The rate of increase of the GNP deflator, which stood above 9.5 percent in 1980–1981, fell to 6 percent in 1982. As measured by the rate of increase in consumer prices, the reduction of inflation was even more spectacular; the rate, which peaked at 13.5 percent in 1980, fell to 10.4 percent in 1981, to 6.1 percent in 1982, and only 1.4 percent in the first semester of 1983 (at annual rate). The real U.S. GDP, which increased at an average annual rate of 2.3 percent in 1974–1980 and by 2 percent in 1981, fell by 1.7 percent in 1982. Unemployment, which stood at 6 percent in 1978–1979, increased to slightly over 7 percent in 1980–1981 before reaching 9.5 percent in 1982.

Thus, at a relatively high cost, inflation was being brought under control in the United States and in most countries of the OECD after a decade of turmoil marked by the oil shocks of 1973 and 1979–1980.

Oil Shocks

The posted price of Saudi Arabian crude oil, which had been $1.80 a barrel throughout the 1960s, was raised between 1971 and early 1973 in three steps to $2.59 a barrel and stood at $3.00 a barrel before the Yom Kippur War in October 1973. In early 1974, the price of a barrel of oil reached $11.65. This price remained almost unchanged for the next five years and so declined by 10 percent in real terms. On December 26, 1978, oil exports from Iran stopped, following strikes against the Shah. The average official Organization of Petroleum Exporting Countries (OPEC) export price, which stood at $12.87 a barrel at the end of 1978, increased to $31.00 a barrel by May 1980. The OECD import price (landed CIF price after six weeks of transportation) increased from $14.00 in 1978 to $32.50 a barrel in June 1980.

By the early 1960s, the OECD was importing about 20 percent of its energy supplies; this proportion increased to 37 percent by 1977, with oil accounting for 95 percent of all net energy imports. The 1973–1974 and 1979–1980 oil price rises represented substantial deteriorations in the terms of trade. Each cost around 2 percent of GNP for the OECD area. The area's net oil import bill rose from about $140 billion in 1978 to an annual rate of $290 billion in the spring of 1980. (By way of comparison, the price cuts in the first half of 1983 led to a decline in the OECD net oil import bill equivalent to 0.4 percent of GNP of the area at an annual rate.)

Structural Changes in the 1960s and 1970s

The oil shocks accelerated structural changes that were under way in the 1960s and 1970s. Industry represents a smaller share of GDP now compared with two decades ago for the seven major industrial countries, as it does for the OECD as a whole (its share in both groups fell from about 40 percent of GDP on average in 1960–1966 to about 38 percent of GDP on average in 1974–1980; see Table 4.4). More strikingly, services, which already represented more than half of GDP in the early 1960s, now account for about 58 percent of GDP in the seven industrial countries and in the OECD.

Since manufacturing activity is more sensitive to business cycles than are services, the swings in activity in the 1980s are more limited than in the 1950s or prior decades. Employment has also shifted from agriculture and industry to services. From the early 1960s to the end of the 1970s, combined employment in agriculture and industry in the OECD countries fell from about 55 percent to about 45 percent while employment in services increased correlatively from 45 to 55 percent (see Table 4.5).

Outlook for Economic Growth

Table 4.6 presents actual statistics for 1980–1982, estimates for 1983, and forecasts for 1984 for growth of the real GNP in the 7 and 21 industrial countries as well as the United States. This forecast assumes that the United States maintains a nonrestrictive monetary policy, that the industrial countries make only marginal efforts to reduce their fiscal deficits, and that Germany and Japan implement neutral economic policies (neither expansionary nor restrictive). Further, it assumes that no major reforms to reduce rigidities in economic structures are attempted but that international trade expands both in volume and in value in 1984 and the international banking system continues to operate normally (without major banking failures or defaults of major debtors). After experiencing slow growth between 1980 and 1982, the major industrialized countries, led by the United States, emerged from the recession in the spring of 1983. Data as of late December 1983 confirmed that the growth in the developed world should exceed 3 percent in 1984, following growth of about 2 percent in 1983. Economists generally accept that growth beyond 1984 will not exceed 4 percent per year even under the most favorable circumstances unless major reforms of the economies of developed countries occur. They also believe that should growth fall below 2 percent, it would reduce the scope for exports from the developing world to the developed world below the minimum level necessary to service the developing world's external debt.[6]

TABLE 4.4   SHARES OF VALUE ADDED IN VARIOUS SECTORS
IN GDP, 1960–1980
(AVERAGE OF PERCENTAGES)

	1960–1966	1967–1973	1974–1980
Seven industrial countries			
Agriculture	5.0	4.0	3.7
Industry	39.9	38.8	37.9
(Manufacturing)	(29.7)	(28.8)	(27.3)
Services	55.1	57.1	58.4
OECD			
Agriculture	5.8	4.6	4.2
Industry	39.6	38.6	37.5
(Manufacturing)	(29.3)	(28.4)	(26.8)
Services	54.6	56.8	58.3

SOURCE: OECD, *Historical Statistics, 1960–1980* (Paris, 1982).

TABLE 4.5   SHARE OF EMPLOYMENT IN VARIOUS SECTORS IN
TOTAL CIVILIAN EMPLOYMENT OF OECD, 1960–1980
(AVERAGE OF PERCENTAGES)

	1960–1966	1967–1973	1974–1980
Agriculture	19.1	14.0	10.9
Industry	36.2	36.6	34.6
(Manufacturing)	(26.9)	(27.3)	(25.3)
Services	44.7	49.4	54.5

SOURCE: OECD, *Historical Statistics, 1960–1980* (Paris, 1982).

TABLE 4.6   GROWTH IN REAL GNP IN SEVERAL GROUPS
OF COUNTRIES, 1980–1984
(IN PERCENTAGE CHANGE FROM PRECEDING YEAR)

	1980	1981	1982	1983	1984
United States	−0.4	1.9	−1.9	3.5	5.0
7 industrial countries	1.1	1.5	−0.5	2.5	3.7
21 industrial countries	1.3	1.2	−0.3	2.2	3.5

SOURCES: IMF, *World Economic Outlook* (Washington, D.C., 1983); and OECD, *Economic Outlook* (Paris, December 1983).

The growth in output of the oil-exporting developing countries obviously depends on oil export revenues. The non-oil developing countries confront major adjustment problems. Both groups of countries are dependent on the evolution of economic activity in the industrial world (see discussion of Table 4.15 below). In spite of the difficulties, real growth in the non-oil developing countries was remarkable until 1980. But the reduction of their export markets and the financial burden of their foreign debts have affected their performance in the 1980s.

Table 4.7 (based on the same assumptions as Table 4.6) presents data on real growth for several groups of countries. The economic growth of the oil-exporting countries, which averaged 6 percent per year after the oil boom of 1973, turned negative in 1980–1982 and was almost zero in 1983. The economic growth of non-oil developing countries (excluding China), which averaged 5 percent per year over 1973–1979, was about 4 percent in 1980; in 1981–1983, it fell below the rate of population growth. The turnaround in economic performance was even sharper for the major exporters of manufactures; their annual rate of growth fell from an average of 6 percent over 1973–1979 to 4.5 percent in 1980 to almost zero in 1981–1983.

The outlook for real world economic growth in 1984–1985 points to a slow recovery in the same environment of suboptimal allocation of scarce resources that has existed since the early 1970s. Even the communist countries have experienced a slowdown in real growth. The average annual rate of growth of the net material product of the members-states of the Council for Mutual Economic Assistance (COMECON) fell from 6.2 percent in 1971–1975 to 4.1 percent in 1976–1980 and is expected to be less than 3 percent in 1981–1985.

The United States is not just the world economic leader; it is above all the regulator (through repercussions of U.S. domestic monetary policy) of the supply of dollars to the world. And the demand for dollars keeps increasing. About 85 percent of the international trade in oil products is financed in dollars, and it is estimated that more than 80 percent of the foreign debt of developing countries is denominated in dollars. Since the value of oil trade expanded considerably after the second oil shock while debt-service payments on the foreign debt of developing countries were increasing at a very high rate until 1982 (see Table 4.11) and should increase again in 1984 without major debt reschedulings, the structural demand for dollars is very large. As the tight U.S. monetary policy until 1982 reduced the rate of growth of the quantity of dollars supplied, real interest rates in the United States and in the world and the exchange rate of the dollar with respect to the other world currencies rose.

Through these channels, the U.S. Federal Reserve can influence international economic activity. The restrictive U.S. monetary policy of the early 1980s reduced the world output of goods and services. The increase in the structural demand for dollars and the increase in uncertainty led to an increase in the *ex ante* demand for real money balances, which was not met until mid-1982 in order to reduce the rate of inflation or disinflate the international economy.

INTERNATIONAL DEBT AND FINANCIAL FLOWS IN THE 1970S AND EARLY 1980S

The evolution of the current account of the balance of payments of the main groups of countries has been marked by the two oil shocks (see Table 4.8). The decline in the current-account surplus of the oil-exporting countries from 1980 to 1982 was remarkable—from a surplus of $114 billion in 1980 to a deficit of $2 billion in 1982. Over the same period, the net position of the industrial countries improved by about $39 billion. The non-oil developing countries' current-account deficit increased from $29 billion in 1977 to $108 billion in 1981; it fell to $87 billion in 1982 and was about $68 billion in 1983 (see Table 4.10 for details).

The non-oil developing countries have had to finance increasing current-account deficits since 1973. The net external borrowing needs of these countries tripled from the average in 1974–1977 to the peak in 1981 (see Table 4.9). The shift in the sources of financing was no less remarkable from 1981 to 1983. The share of official sources in net borrowing was expected to increase from 35 percent in 1981 to 69 percent in 1983. Both the trade balance and balance on net services and private transfers of the non-oil developing countries were negative (see Table 4.10). The deficit in the trade balance more than doubled from an annual average of $36 billion in 1974–1979 to $77 billion in 1980–1981 before falling to $47 billion in 1982–1983. The deficit in the balance on net services and private transfers increased from an annual average of $5.5 billion in 1974–1979 to $21 billion in 1980–1981 to $30.5 billion in 1982–1983.

Although the reduction from 1981 to 1983 in the aggregate current-account deficit of the non-oil developing countries was estimated to be $40 billion, this improvement "represented a response to extreme financial pressures, rather than a more comfortable balance between underlying payments and receipts."[7] This applied especially to the non-oil trade balance.

The increase in the external debt of the non-oil developing countries and in the cost to service it is illustrated in Table 4.11. The total debt increased from $130 billion in 1973 to almost $400 billion in 1979 to over

TABLE 4.7   GROWTH IN REAL GNP IN SEVERAL GROUPS
            OF DEVELOPING COUNTRIES, 1968–1983
            (PERCENTAGES)

	AVERAGE 1968–1972	AVERAGE 1973–1979	CHANGE FROM PRECEDING YEAR 1980	1981	1982	1983
Oil-exporting countries	9.0	6.0	−2.3	−4.3	−4.8	—
Non-oil-exporting countries (including China)	n.a.	n.a.	4.8	2.5	1.4	2.3
Non-oil-exporting countries (excluding China)	6.0	5.0	4.3	2.4	0.9	1.9
Major exporters of manufactures	8.0	6.0	4.5	−0.2	0.2	0.4

SOURCE: IMF, *World Economic Outlook* (Washington, D.C., 1983).

TABLE 4.8   CURRENT ACCOUNTS OF SEVERAL GROUPS
            OF COUNTRIES, 1973–1983
            (IN BILLIONS OF U.S. DOLLARS)

	21 industrial countries	Oil-exporting countries	Non-oil developing countries
1973	20.3	6.7	− 11.3
1974	− 10.8	68.3	− 37.0
1975	19.8	35.4	− 46.3
1976	0.5	40.3	− 32.6
1977	− 2.2	30.2	− 28.9
1978	32.7	2.2	− 41.3
1979	− 5.6	68.6	− 61.0
1980	− 40.1	114.3	− 89.0
1981	0.6	65.0	− 107.7
1982	− 1.2	− 2.2	− 86.8
1983	16.0	− 27.0	− 68.0

SOURCE: IMF, *World Economic Outlook* (Washington, D.C., 1983).

NOTE: Current accounts on goods, services, and private transfers. The net current-account positions of the various groups of countries do not add to zero even when non-IMF members are included in the world total. In the judgment of the IMF staff (ibid., p. 166), the "rise in the global current account asymmetry appears to have been lodged in types of transactions that are conducted chiefly by residents of the industrial and oil-exporting countries."

TABLE 4.9   FINANCING OF CURRENT-ACCOUNT DEFICITS AND
RESERVE ACCRETIONS OF THE NON-OIL
DEVELOPING COUNTRIES, 1974–1983
(IN BILLIONS OF U.S. DOLLARS)

	Average 1974–1977	Average 1978–1980	1981	1982	1983
Current-account deficit	36	64	108	87	68
Use of reserves[a]	−7	−11	−2	7	−7
Non-debt-creating flows[b]	13	22	28	25	24
Net external borrowing	30	53	82	55	51
(From private sources)	(18)	(37)	(53)	(24)	(16)
(From official sources)	(12)	(16)	(29)	(31)	(35)

SOURCE: IMF, *World Economic Outlook* (Washington, D.C., 1983).
[a]Negative sign indicates accumulation of reserves.
[b]Includes official transfers, SDR allocations, valuation adjustments, gold monetization, and direct investment flows.

TABLE 4.10   SELECTED COMPONENTS OF BALANCES ON CURRENT ACCOUNTS
OF THE NON-OIL DEVELOPING COUNTRIES, 1973–1983
(IN BILLIONS OF U.S. DOLLARS)

	BALANCE ON CURRENT ACCOUNT	TRADE BALANCE			NET SERVICES AND PRIVATE TRANSFERS
		Oil-trade	Non-oil	Total	
1973	− 11.3	− 3.8	− 6.5	−10.3	− 1.0
1974	− 37.0	−13.9	−19.4	−33.3	− 3.7
1975	− 46.3	−13.9	−26.9	−40.8	− 5.5
1976	− 32.6	−17.1	−10.0	−27.0	− 5.6
1977	− 28.9	−18.4	− 6.8	−25.3	− 3.7
1978	− 41.3	−18.6	−18.0	−36.6	− 4.7
1979	− 61.0	−25.2	−26.1	−51.3	− 9.7
1980	− 89.0	−38.7	−35.6	−74.3	−14.7
1981	−107.7	−37.3	−42.3	−79.6	−28.1
1982	− 86.8	−30.0	−22.2	−52.2	−34.6
1983	− 67.8	−25.1	−16.4	−41.4	−26.4

SOURCE: IMF, *World Economic Outlook* (Washington, D.C., 1983).

$660 billion in 1983 (the share of short-term debt remained below 20 percent). As a percentage of GDP, the total debt represented about 28 percent in 1977–1980, 31 percent in 1981, and about 35 percent in 1982–1983. The value of debt-service payments doubled from $25 billion in 1975 (or 16 percent of exports of goods and services) to $50 billion in 1978 (19 percent), doubling again to $107 billion in 1982 (24 percent). The reduction in the percentage of service payments on exports of goods and services from 1982 to 1983 was almost entirely due to the rescheduling of some $20 billion of debt obligations that fell due in 1983; without this, the percentage of service payments would have been 23.3 instead of 19.3 in 1983.

Although the debt-service ratio or percentage of debt-service payments on exports of goods and services increased from 14.4 percent in 1974 to 20.4 percent in 1981 for the non-oil developing countries as a group, its evolution differed considerably among the various regions of the world. The debt-service ratio increased moderately in Asia (from 7.8 percent in 1974 to 9.2 percent in 1981) and in the Middle East (from 14.4 percent in 1974 to 17.5 percent in 1981); it increased substantially in Africa (from 6.7 percent in 1974 to 15.2 percent in 1981) and the Western Hemisphere (from 27.9 percent in 1974 to 41.7 percent in 1981). Then the debt-service ratio shot up to 54.0 percent in 1982 in the Western Hemisphere, leading to the near simultaneous default of Mexico, Argentina, and Brazil. In that same year, it was 20.1 percent in Africa, 9.8 percent in Asia, and 17.6 percent in the Middle East. Moreover, while in 1982 short-term debt represented 18.4 percent of the total outstanding debt of non-oil developing countries, it was only 11.0 percent in Africa, 13.0 percent in the Middle East, and 18.5 percent in Asia but reached 22.6 percent in the Western Hemisphere, rendering the countries of that region very vulnerable to changes in market perceptions of lending risks. Finally, while in 1982 the share of the long-term external debt of the non-oil developing countries owed to private financial institutions (essentially commercial banks) was 43.0 percent, it was 34.7 percent in Africa, 28.7 percent in Asia, and only 12.5 percent in the Middle East but reached 54.8 percent in the Western Hemisphere. Since the Western Hemisphere owed almost $210 million in long-term debt alone in 1982 (see Table 4.12), the risk of a default of that continent to the commercial banks becomes clear.

The exposure of the international banking sector to developing countries' debt has received wide publicity. The Bank for International Settlements (BIS) collects statistics on claims and liabilities of banks in an area comprising the Group of Ten countries (the seven industrial countries, the Netherlands, Belgium, and Sweden); Austria, Denmark, Ireland, Luxembourg, and Switzerland; and the offshore branches of U.S. banks in the

TABLE 4.11   NON-OIL DEVELOPING COUNTRIES: EXTERNAL DEBT, 1973–1983

	1973	1974	1975	1976	1977	1978	1979	1980	1981	1982	1983
Total Amount and in Relation to Exports and GDP											
Amount of external debt (billions of dollars)	130.1	160.8	190.8	228.0	278.5	336.3	396.9	474.0	555.0	612.4	664.3
Short-term (less than 1 year)	(18.4)	(22.7)	(27.3)	(33.2)	(42.5)	(49.7)	(58.8)	(85.5)	(102.2)	(112.7)	(92.4)
Long-term (more than 1 year)	(111.8)	(138.1)	(163.5)	(194.9)	(235.9)	(286.6)	(338.1)	(388.5)	(452.8)	(499.6)	(571.6)
As percentage of exports of goods and services[a]	115.4	104.6	122.4	125.5	126.4	130.2	119.2	112.9	124.9	143.3	144.4
As percentage of GDP[a]	22.4	21.8	23.8	25.7	27.4	28.5	27.5	27.6	31.0	34.7	34.7
External Debt-Service Payments[b]											
Value of debt-service payments (billions of dollars)	17.9	22.1	25.1	27.8	34.7	50.3	65.0	76.2	94.7	107.1	93.2
Interest payments	(6.9)	(9.3)	(10.5)	(10.9)	(13.6)	(19.4)	(28.0)	(40.4)	(55.1)	(59.2)	(55.1)
Amortization	(11.1)	(12.8)	(14.6)	(16.8)	(21.1)	(30.9)	(36.9)	(35.8)	(39.7)	(47.9)	(38.1)
Service payments as percentage of export of goods and services	15.9	14.4	16.1	15.3	15.4	19.0	19.0	17.6	20.4	23.9	19.3

SOURCE: IMF, *World Economic Outlook* (Washington, D.C., 1983).

[a]Ratio of year-end debt to exports or GDP for year indicated.

[b]On short-term and long-term external debt, taking into account rescheduling agreements in 1982 and early 1983.

Bahamas, the Cayman Islands, Hong Kong, Panama, and Singapore. Table 4.13 presents the claims and liabilities of the banks in the BIS reporting area with respect to the non-oil developing countries. Clearly the exposure of the banks in the BIS reporting area with respect to the non-oil developing countries is growing (the claims on Argentina, Brazil, and Mexico reached a total of $137.6 billion at the end of 1982).

At the end of 1982, interbank deposits (between the banks of the BIS area) represented $667 billion out of total external claims of the banks in the BIS area of $1,687 billion. Interbank deposits represented $600 billion out of total external liabilities of $1,620 billion (net of interbank deposits, claims and liabilities were both equal to $1,020 billion). The fragility of the international banking system is evident—a large share of bank resources consists of deposits by other banks that might be withdrawn at short notice. These interbank deposits could easily play the role of a "panic multiplier." Since the claims (or credits) of the banks in the BIS area on the non-oil developing countries represented $306.1 billion out of $1,020 billion of claims (net of interbank deposits), what would happen if some large borrowers defaulted is clear. First, some banks with high exposure, the first ring, would lose a large part of their assets. Second, and literally in minutes, the other banks would withdraw part of their deposits to protect themselves. The banks of the first ring could find themselves without liquid or short-term resources and would be bankrupt. A second ring of banks with large remaining deposits in the banks of the first ring would fail. And so on, until the complete collapse of the international banking system.

THE EVOLUTION OF INTERNATIONAL TRADE, 1960–1983

The non-oil developing countries will be able to service their debts as long as their exports grow. Between 1963 and 1973, world output (excluding construction and services) rose by 6 percent annually, and the volume of world trade by 8.5 percent annually. Over the period 1974–1980, output growth fell by half to 3 percent annually and the annual rate of growth of trade by almost half to about 5 percent. In 1981–1983, it is estimated that output and world trade growth decreased further to 1 percent annually. Exports of goods by the non-oil developing countries rose by 6.7 percent over the period 1963–1972 and by slightly less than 5.0 percent per year over the period 1973–1983.

International trade rose faster than output in the 1960s and 1970s, and the share of exports in output has been increasing regularly. This is illustrated in Table 4.14, which presents the evolution of the share of exports of goods and services in GDP for several groups of industrial countries. The

TABLE 4.12 SOURCES OF EXTERNAL FINANCING OF NON-OIL
DEVELOPING COUNTRIES, 1978–1983
(IN BILLIONS OF U.S. DOLLARS)

	1978	1979	1980	1981	1982	1983
Total outstanding debt	336.3	396.9	474.0	555.0	612.4	664.3
Short-term debt	49.7	58.8	85.5	102.2	112.7	92.6
Long-term debt	286.6	338.1	388.5	452.8	499.6	571.7
To Western Hemisphere	(114.3)	(135.1)	(154.7)	(192.6)	(208.9)	(247.4)
Official creditors	117.5	133.0	152.9	172.4	193.2	218.7
Private creditors	169.1	205.1	235.6	280.4	306.4	353.0
Guaranteed debt	(112.7)	(137.8)	(158.1)	(183.7)	(202.2)	(239.3)

SOURCE: IMF, *World Economic Outlook* (Washington, D.C., 1983).

TABLE 4.13 CLAIMS AND LIABILITIES OF BANKS IN THE BIS AREA WITH
RESPECT TO NON-OIL DEVELOPING COUNTRIES, 1978–1982
(IN BILLIONS OF U.S. DOLLARS, YEAR-END TOTALS)

	1978	1979	1980	1981	1982
Claims	155.0	195.4	241.3	285.6	306.1
Liabilities	91.6	105.4	112.5	117.9	120.2

SOURCE: Quarterly Reports, Bank for International Settlements.

TABLE 4.14 SHARE OF EXPORTS OF GOODS AND SERVICES
IN GDP, 1960–1980
(PERCENTAGES)

	1960–1966	1967–1973	1974–1980	1979	1980
United States	5.1	5.6	8.7	9.0	10.1
7 industrial countries	9.7	11.1	15.8	16.3	17.5
EEC	19.6	22.2	28.3	28.9	29.3
OECD	11.6	13.3	18.3	19.0	20.2

SOURCE: OECD, *Historical Statistics, 1960–1980* (Paris, 1982).

share of exports in GDP doubled in the United States from 5.1 percent in the early 1960s to 10.1 percent in 1980, and it almost doubled in the OECD countries as a group over the same period, from 11.6 to 20.2 percent. The increase in the openness of the economies of the industrial countries is remarkable. This openness continued to rise after the oil shocks as exports grew in order to pay for increased oil imports; the share of exports of the industrial countries going to the oil-exporting countries increased from 4 percent in 1973 to 9.5 percent in 1981 (see Table 4.15).

Table 4.15 shows clearly the importance of the industrial countries in the export trade of the oil-exporting and the non-oil developing countries alike. The share of exports of the oil-exporting countries going to the industrial countries was about 73 percent in 1980–1981; the corresponding share for the non-oil developing countries was about 57 percent. (The intra-trade of industrial countries in 1981 covered 65.1 percent of their exports and 63.7 percent of their imports). When the rate of growth of output in the industrial countries diminishes, the exports of the non-oil developing countries are directly affected.

To better understand the 1970s, we need to deal with a final question: Given the magnitude of the oil shock in 1973, how did the world avoid another Great Depression?

THE U.S. GREAT RECESSION

From the peak of activity in the fourth quarter of 1973 to the trough of the U.S. recession in the first quarter of 1975, real GNP fell by 4.8 percent. While activity just slowed at first, real GNP plunged in the last quarter of 1974 and in the first quarter of 1975 at an annual rate of almost 7 percent; the real gross product of the goods sector fell at an annual rate of 12 percent, and real gross private domestic investment fell at an annual rate of 50 percent over the same six-month period. These rates of decline were of the same order of magnitude as those recorded at the beginning of the Great Depression.

The sense of panic that developed in the winter of 1974–1975 after the oil shock (and the five-month oil embargo of the preceding winter) at a time of double-digit inflation and interest rates, skyrocketing unemployment (up 54 percent from 1974 to 1975), and a large stock market decline is comparable to the state of shock that prevailed after the stock market crash of October 1929. But whereas 1930 was only the beginning of the Depression, the U.S. economy recovered in the spring of 1975.

What factors contributed to the crisis?

TABLE 4.15   DIRECTION OF EXPORT FLOWS (GOODS), 1973–1981
(PERCENTAGES OF TOTAL EXPORTS)

	1973	1974	1975	1976	1977	1978	1979	1980	1981
Industrial countries (21)*									
Industrial countries	72.4	69.1	65.5	67.6	67.3	67.0	69.0	67.5	65.1
Oil-exporting countries	4.0	5.3	8.1	8.4	9.1	9.0	7.1	7.9	9.5
Non-oil developing countries	18.3	20.2	19.9	17.9	18.1	18.7	18.8	19.4	20.3
Oil-exporting countries									
Industrial countries	77.7	76.9	74.9	73.5	74.0	75.7	74.7	73.6	72.5
Oil-exporting countries	0.7	0.4	1.0	0.9	1.0	1.1	1.3	1.4	1.5
Non-oil developing countries	19.3	19.9	20.8	21.5	21.3	20.5	21.5	22.5	23.2
Non-oil developing countries									
Industrial countries	61.7	60.9	58.1	61.2	60.0	60.0	59.7	56.7	56.6
Oil-exporting countries	3.1	4.6	5.8	5.6	6.5	6.2	5.6	6.1	7.1
Non-oil developing countries	21.9	22.2	22.2	21.5	21.7	22.1	23.3	24.3	23.8

SOURCE: IMF, *International Financial Statistics, Supplement on Trade Statistics* (Washington, D.C., 1982).

*Columns do not add to 100 due to omission of countries that do not fall into categories listed.

Between the beginning of 1964 and the summer of 1965, the U.S. involvement in Vietnam increased considerably. President Johnson refused to raise taxes in January 1966, and government deficits and the public debt rose sizably. The war expenditure buoyed the economy, and inflation accelerated. Otto Eckstein, using simulations performed on the Data Resources (DRI) Econometric Model of the U.S. economy, reports that

> the Vietnam War was the decisive economic event for the period 1965–1972. Without the War, a good expansion could have proceeded over that entire interval . . . capital formation would have been substantially higher and the recession of 1970–71 would have been avoided.
>
> But beginning in 1973, the War ceased to be the determinant of the economy. Food, energy, inflation, and tight money took over.[8]

He then analyzes the respective contributions of the causes of the 1974–1975 recession:

1. The monetary and fiscal policies of the ten years preceding the recession, which were needlessly volatile and gave a series of shocks to the private economy that repeatedly disrupted the normal growth process;
2. The food price explosion of 1972–1974 following a series of natural disasters and policy errors;
3. The devaluations of the dollar in 1971 and 1973;
4. The coincidence of the business cycle upswings of all the industrial nations in 1972–1973;
5. The price controls in various phases from August 15, 1971, to April 30, 1974, which distorted the structure of relative prices;
6. The oil embargo of November 1973 and the large increases in the price of oil.

Eckstein estimates that more than half of the unemployment rate in 1975 is explained by these factors; the energy crisis accounts for 22 percent of the unemployment rate, the monetary policies of 1964–1975 for 19 percent, and the other factors for 12 percent. He concludes:

> The double-digit inflation of 1974 and the Great Recession of 1975 were caused by the unhappy coincidence of the energy and food shocks, and by extreme and unstable monetary policies. Excessive ease of monetary policy in 1971–72 helped create the excessive investment boom and over-optimistic expectations. When monetary policy sought to freeze the money supply during the worst of the price shocks, a financial crisis was created which was the worst since the Great Depression.[9]

TABLE 4.16   EVOLUTION OF SOME U.S. AGGREGATES, 1971–1976
(PERCENTAGE CHANGE FROM PRECEDING PERIOD)

	$M2^a$	GDP^b	X^c
1971	10.5	3.3	0.7
1972	10.1	5.6	9.2
1973	5.2	5.5	25.5
1974	4.6	−0.7	11.5
1975	10.2	−0.9	−4.5
1976	12.5	5.3	6.3

SOURCES: IMF, international financial statistics in 1982 *Yearbook*; and U.S. Department of Commerce, NIPA, September 1981.
[a]End-of-period stocks.
[b]Real GDP.
[c]Real exports of goods and services.

How then was a depression avoided in 1975?

Table 4.16 presents the evolution of some relevant aggregates. As previously mentioned, monetary policy contributed largely to the recession of 1974–1975, but it became very expansionary in 1975. The federal funds rate fell from 12.9 percent in July 1974 to 5.2 percent in March 1975. Exports were buoyant in 1974 and helped to compensate for the strict monetary policy effect on output. By the time exports fell in 1975, monetary policy had become expansionary. Finally, both exports and the money stock increased sizably in 1976. In total from 1973 to 1976, the stock of money increased by 30 percent and exports by 13 percent in real terms. Two additional reasons explain the end of the decline: unemployment insurance benefits rose and helped maintain consumption, and fiscal policy became expansionary when taxes were reduced in the last three quarters of 1975.

Obviously the dramatic difference between the Great Depression and the Great Recession is that during the former both the domestic financial system and the international economy crashed while during the latter, over 1975–1976, both monetary policy and the international economy pulled the U.S. private sector out of a crisis that they had largely caused. As a matter of fact, monetary policy became too lax in 1976 and helped bring a return of inflation.

The growth of output and international trade slowed after the first oil shock but not just because of it; the slowdown in productivity increases accounts for most of the reduction in real output. The United States embarked on a restrictive monetary policy course in the fall of 1979, and after the usual lags, output growth slowed. International trade stopped growing, at a time when the foreign debt of the non-oil developing countries kept increasing. Before trying to anticipate future economic developments, let us review the monetary and fiscal policies of the leading industrial countries, which still appear to hold the key to the future economic progress of the world.

5

Monetary, Fiscal, and Trade Policies of the Industrial Countries

This chapter first develops a simple analytical framework to establish the interdependence of fiscal policy (and the size of the budget deficits), the current account of the balance of payments, and the evolution of the stock of money and shows that large budget deficits strongly affect the overall economic situation. Actual monetary and fiscal policies are reviewed next.

ANALYTICAL FRAMEWORK

In a financial system, banks hold assets (reserves $[RS]$ and credits $[CR]$ and have liabilities (demand $[De]$ and time $[Ti]$ deposits); the central bank holds assets (gold and foreign currency $[NFA]$, refinancing by discounting bills $[RE]$ and net credits to the public sector $[CPUB]$) and has liabilities (currency holdings of the public $[Cp]$ and bank reserves $[RS]$). To consolidate the balance sheet (Table 5.1) of the financial system, the banking system (banks plus central bank) holds assets (net foreign assets $[NFA]$, bank credits $[CR]$, refinancing $[RE]$, and central bank credits to the public sector $[CPUB]$) and has liabilities (currency $[Cp]$ held by the public [nonbank private sector] and deposits $[De, Ti]$).

The sum of the liabilities is the money supply, equal to money ($M1 = Cp + De$) and quasi-money (Ti). The stock of money is also equal to the sum of net foreign assets and total domestic credit. Changes in net foreign assets are equal to the deficit or surplus of the overall balance of payments. Hence the balance on foreign operations affects the stock of money directly.

The balance of payments is the sum of the current account and certain elements of the capital account (depending on where the financing line is drawn). The balance on current account is the difference between exports

TABLE 5.1   BALANCE SHEET OF THE BANKING SYSTEM

Assets	*Liabilities*
NFA + (CR + RE) + CPUB	Cp + De + Ti
M2 = counterparts of money supply	M2 = money and quasi-money

NOTE: Ignoring, for purposes of exposition, nonmonetary liabilities of the banking system such as capital and reserves, as well as noncredit assets.

and imports of goods and services, or net exports of goods and services (NX). In national income accounting, the gross product (Y) of goods and services of an economy is equal to the sum of consumption (C), investment (I), government spending (G), and net exports (NX):

$$Y = C + I + G + NX. \tag{1}$$

The gross product is also equal to the sum of disposable income (Y_d) plus taxes (T), less net transfers (R):

$$Y = Y_d + T - R \tag{2}$$

while disposable income is the sum of consumption (C) and saving (S):

$$Y_d = C + S. \tag{3}$$

Hence, combining identities (1), (2), and (3) yields the fundamental national income accounting identity:

$$C + I + G + NX = C + S + T - R \tag{4}$$

which can be simplified and rewritten as

$$S - \dot{I} = (G + R - T) + NX. \tag{5}$$

Therefore, the excess of saving over investment of the private sector $(S - \dot{I})$ is equal to the budget deficit $(G + R - T)$ plus net exports (NX). Hence if the private sector is in equilibrium, a budget deficit will automatically entail a corresponding deficit on the current account of the balance of payments (excess of imports over exports). This will be true whatever the source of financing of the government. For example, by borrowing abroad, the government simply finances the current-account deficit that it created; if the private sector is in equilibrium, the difference between the government deficit and its borrowing abroad will be financed by net private capital inflows or losses of net foreign assets. If there are private capital outflows and if net foreign assets are kept constant, there will be an excess supply of domestic currency with respect to foreign currency, and the domestic currency will depreciate.

From Accounting to Economics

Although the fundamental accounting identity (equation 5 above) is always true, the discussion above assumes equality between saving and investment in the private sector and emphasizes the automatic consequence of budget deficits on current-account deficits and the effects of budget financing through foreign borrowing or domestic money creation. Alternatively, in an economic analysis, the government can attract the savings of the private sector by raising interest rates and hence crowd private borrowers out of financial markets. Investment will be reduced by the inability of the private sector to compete with the government on the terms set by the national treasury, and the excess of saving over investment of the private sector will finance the public sector deficit and reduce the impact of the government deficit on the external sector at the cost of a reduced capital accumulation and future growth.

Hence, government deficits have the following consequences depending on the monetary policy followed: (1) if monetary policy does not allow the financing of the deficit through money creation, the share of the budget deficit not financed by the private sector will cause and be equal to the current-account deficit. Reduced investment will reduce future growth, and the financing of the current-account deficit will entail an increase in foreign debt; and (2) if the deficit is financed through money creation, the increase in money supply will fuel inflation.

Naturally, government deficits can be financed by any combination of borrowing from the private and foreign sectors and money creation. The consequences of these various forms of financing will depend on the willingness (and hence expectations) of the domestic and foreign economic agents to hold government debt. Depending on these expectations, the same financing mix might entail different effects on interest and exchange rates.

The crucial point is that government deficits have many more consequences than just the alleged impact on economic activity through the Keynesian multiplier. Although government deficits do generally increase activity in the short-term, the medium-term impact will depend on the mode of financing as well as on the willingness of the private and foreign sectors to hold government debt. Contemporary governments have found that the medium-term impact can be negative.

Actual Policies

Monetary Policies

Monetary policy has been given the primary role in containing the growth of nominal demand in the industrial countries since 1979. At the same time, the principal target of monetary policy shifted from interest rates to quantitative limits on monetary aggregates.

The evidence of the shift to a policy of monetary restraint can be found in the evolution of nominal and real monetary aggregates as well as nominal and real interest rates (see Table 5.2). Both before and after the shift to

TABLE 5.2   SEVEN INDUSTRIAL COUNTRIES: MONETARY POLICIES, 1976–1982 (ANNUAL PERCENTAGE CHANGES, EXCEPT AS NOTED)[a]

	1976	1977	1978	1979	1980	1981	1982
Real GNP	5.3	4.3	4.5	3.5	1.1	1.5	−0.4
GNP deflator	7.1	7.1	7.3	8.0	9.1	8.5	6.7
Nominal value of GNP	12.8	11.8	12.1	11.8	10.3	10.1	6.3
Nominal monetary aggregates[b]							
Narrow money (M1)	8.0	10.5	11.5	7.3	5.6	6.5	8.5
Broad money (M2 or M3)	13.6	11.8	10.9	9.9	9.8	9.8	9.5
Real monetary aggregates [b,c]							
Narrow money (M1)	0.9	3.3	3.6	−0.5	−3.5	−1.6	2.7
Broad money (M2 or M3)	5.5	4.6	3.0	2.0	0.3	1.5	3.5
Nominal interest rates (percentage per annum)							
Short-term	6.9	6.4	6.8	9.2	11.7	13.3	10.9
Long-term	8.8	8.2	8.3	9.3	11.3	13.2	12.4
Real interest rates[d] (percentage per annum)							
Short-term	−0.3	−0.6	−0.3	1.2	2.4	4.2	4.0
Long-term	1.5	1.1	1.0	1.3	2.0	4.2	5.4

SOURCE: IMF, *World Economic Outlook* (Washington, D.C., 1983).

[a]Data are in terms of weighted averages.

[b]End-of-period money stocks.

[c]Deflated by GNP deflators.

[d]Difference between nominal rate and changes in GNP deflator.

stricter monetary policies, there were wide differences among countries. As emphasized in Chapter 4, U.S. monetary policies remained very strict in 1981, and the small relative increase in the combined monetary aggregates from 1980 to 1981 is attributable to Japan and France. The United States allowed its money supply to increase faster after mid-1982 than in the previous two years. But measured by real interest rates, monetary policy remained restrictive. Real long-term interest rates for the seven industrial countries increased from 1 percent in 1978 to 2 percent in 1980 to 5.4 percent in 1982.

Fiscal Policies and Social Transfers

The growth of government spending as a share of GDP accelerated markedly in the industrial countries in the 1960s and early 1970s. After the oil shock of 1973, it kept increasing rapidly in the major European countries and Japan but less in the United States. Total government outlays as a percentage of GDP increased in the United States from 27.8 percent of GDP in 1960 and 31.2 percent in 1973 to 33.2 percent in 1980. In the seven industrial countries (including the United States), they increased from 28.9 percent of GDP in 1960 and 32.9 percent in 1973 to 38.3 percent in 1980 (see Table 5.3). While spending on goods and services as a share of GDP remained almost unchanged over the whole period, the growth of transfers, subsidies, and interest payments was extraordinary; for the seven industrial countries, transfers and other payments increased from 10.4 percent of GDP in 1960 to 13.5 percent in 1973 to 17.8 percent in 1980.

Ratios of percentage changes in public expenditure to corresponding percentage changes in nominal GDP for selected periods are given in Table 5.4. It appears that for the seven industrial countries, the rate of growth in public expenditure, which was almost 1.3 times the rate of growth in nominal GDP in 1965–1969, was 1.1 times the GDP growth in 1969–1973 before accelerating again to 1.3 times the GDP rate in 1973–1980. But while the high ratio of 1965–1969 was due to the high rate of growth of public expenditure in the United States, the return to this high ratio in 1973–1980 was due to the high rate of growth of public expenditure in Europe and Japan. (See Table 5.4. Data for Japan are not included in Table 5.4 because they do not cover exactly the same public expenditure; for that slightly different definition, the ratios of rate of growth in Japan corresponding to Table 5.4 are 0.92 in 1965–1969, 1.42 in 1969–1973, and 1.90 in 1973–1980). The data for France are given separately to illustrate the impact of the policies of different administrations on this ratio: in 1969–1973 France was governed by President Georges Pompidou, in 1974–1980 by President Valéry Giscard d'Estaing.

TABLE 5.3   GOVERNMENT SPENDING AS PERCENTAGE OF GDP, 1960–1980

	PURCHASES OF GOODS AND SERVICES		TRANSFERS, SUBSIDIES AND INTEREST PAYMENTS		GROSS CAPITAL FORMATION		TOTAL OUTLAYS	
	United States	7 industrial countries	United States	7 industrial countries	United States	7 industrial countries	United States	7 industrial countries
1960	16.9	15.5	8.6	10.4	2.3	3.0	27.8	28.9
1970	19.2	16.7	10.9	12.4	2.1	3.5	32.2	32.6
1973	17.7	15.9	12.0	13.5	1.5	3.5	31.2	32.9
1974	18.3	16.6	12.9	14.6	1.7	3.6	32.9	34.8
1975	18.9	17.5	14.6	16.7	1.9	3.8	35.4	38.0
1976	18.5	17.1	14.5	16.7	1.4	3.4	34.4	37.2
1977	18.0	16.7	14.3	16.9	1.2	3.2	33.5	36.8
1978	17.4	16.2	14.4	17.4	1.3	3.7	33.1	37.3
1979	17.4	16.3	14.1	17.6	1.3	3.6	32.8	37.5
1980	18.1	17.0	13.6	17.8	1.5	3.5	33.2	38.3

SOURCES: OECD, *Historical Statistics, 1960–1980* (Paris, 1982); and idem, *National Accounts, 1963–1980*, vol. 2 (Paris, 1982).

Government spending increased further in 1981–1982, and fiscal deficits rose. Table 5.5 reports historical data, estimates for 1983, and OECD forecasts for 1984 of the financial balances of governments (including local public authorities and transfers) in the industrial countries. For the seven

TABLE 5.4   CHANGES IN RELATIONSHIPS OF PUBLIC EXPENDITURE
TO NOMINAL GDP, 1965–1980
(RATIOS OF RATE OF GROWTH)

	1965–1969	1969–1973	1973–1980
7 industrial countries	1.29	1.12	1.31
United States	1.40	1.06	1.12
United Kingdom, France, Germany, Italy	1.11	1.13	1.33
France	1.10	0.93	1.35

SOURCE: OECD, *National Accounts, 1963–1980*, vol. 2 (Paris, 1982).

TABLE 5.5   FISCAL DATA: SEVEN INDUSTRIAL COUNTRIES, 1978–1984

	1978	1979	1980	1981	1982	1983	1984
General Government Financial Balances, 1978–1984 (surplus [+] or deficit [−] as percentage of nominal GDP/GNP)							
United States	+ 0.2	+ 0.6	− 1.2	− 0.9	− 3.8	− 3.8	− 3.7
Japan	− 5.5	− 4.8	− 4.5	− 4.0	− 4.1	− 3.4	− 2.5
7 industrial countries	− 2.2	− 1.7	− 2.4	− 2.5	− 4.1	− 4.1	− 3.8

SOURCE: OECD, *Economic Outlook* (Paris, 1983).

	1978	1979	1980	1981	1982	1983	1984
General Government Financial Deficits (+) or surplus (−), 1978–1984 (as percentage of gross private savings)							
United States	− 1.1	− 3.5	+ 7.2	+ 5.3	+22.2	+22.2	+21.1
Japan	+18.2	+16.6	+15.6	+14.0	+15.0	+13.1	+ 9.8
7 industrial countries	+ 8.6	+ 6.3	+11.0	+11.5	+20.6	+20.9	+19.2

SOURCE: OECD, *Economic Outlook* (Paris, 1983).

industrial countries, the public deficit increased from an annual average of 2.2 percent of GDP in 1978–1981 to 4.0 percent of GDP in 1982–1984. These deficits take a growing share of gross private savings and crowd out private borrowers. In the seven industrial countries, the public deficit as a share of gross private savings increased from an annual average of 9.4 percent in 1978–1981 to an estimated 20.2 percent in 1982–1984.

It is clear that a reversal of this escalation of deficits is an essential condition for facilitating the financing of private domestic investment activity and hence for helping restore earlier rates of increase in productivity and total output.

THE RISE IN PROTECTIONISM IN THE 1970S AND EARLY 1980S

For three decades before the conclusion of the Tokyo Round of Multilateral Trade Negotiations (MTN) in 1979, trade liberalization allowed a remarkable expansion of international trade: the volume of world trade of goods increased by 8.5 percent annually from 1963 to 1973 and further rose by 5 percent annually in the period 1974–1980 in spite of the slowdown in the growth of world output. But many protectionist measures have been taken or strengthened, especially since 1980, and presently affect more than one-fifth of world trade in manufactures and a third of international trade in agriculture.

Further, and potentially more destructive, attitudes of governments and large segments of the public toward trade have altered, and the main preoccupation has become the balancing of bilateral trade accounts between the major trading countries. An interesting IMF study reviews the protectionist barriers affecting world trade in manufactures and agricultural products.[1] Trade in manufactures accounts for 55 percent of world trade and 70 percent of trade among industrial countries. The average annual growth rate of world exports of manufactured products fell from 11 percent in 1963–1973 to 5 percent in 1974–1980 to 3 percent in 1981.

Automobiles, which account for 8 percent of world trade in manufactures, have been particularly affected by the trend of increased protectionism. Orderly marketing agreements and other forms of restraints now cover two-thirds of Japan's exports of automobiles.

International trade in iron and steel, which accounts for 4 percent of world trade, was restricted in 1981–1983 by major actions of the EEC and the United States. The EEC limits its own output as well as imports through administrative price and quantity determinations. The United States is imposing countervailing duties on subsidized imports. On July 5, 1983,

President Reagan imposed quotas and tariff increases on imports of specialty steel products.

The Multifiber Arrangement, which restricts imports of textile and clothing in the industrial countries, was extended in December 1981 until July 1986. By that date, multilaterally negotiated restrictions in textiles and clothing will have existed for a quarter of a century.

Many of the sectoral pressures for import restrictions in the United States and Europe have been directed toward Japanese exports. Japan's performance in automobiles and consumer electronics is a tribute to the flexibility of its economy and its ability to shift resources to serve new consumer demands, but its success in these areas has led to calls by affected groups in other countries to contain imports of Japanese goods.

Particularly difficult in relation to trade in manufactures is the issue of domestic subsidies, which have increased considerably in the past fifteen years (see above). It is often impossible to separate the effect of subsidies designed to support ailing industries from export subsidies.

With respect to agricultural trade, all the major trading nations are trying to achieve domestic self-sufficiency or security of supply as well as a fair income for the domestic farm sector at a reasonable cost to consumers. These objectives cannot all be attained without resorting to quotas, subsidies, and tariffs. The IMF study focuses on five agricultural commodities—dairy products, fats and oils, grains, meats, and sugar—and shows that "virtually all major industrial countries protect their domestic agricultural sectors to a considerable extent." It also notes that "domestic prices in the European Community exceed 'international' prices by 25–50 percent for beef, lamb, sheep meat, and wheat, and by up to 100 percent for maize and sugar. In Japan, price differentials prevail in the 25–50 percent range for wheat and barley and in the 100–200 percent range for rice, soybeans, sugar, and beef."[2] The United States reimposed (for the first time since 1974) country-specific quotas on imports of sugar, on May 5, 1982, and U.S. import restrictions on beef have passed the burden of adjustment in this strongly cyclical market to foreign suppliers.

The list of restrictions on agricultural trade is long and only mirrors the priority national policies give to the achievement of domestic social and political objectives over efficiency and trade liberalization.

The rise in protectionism in recent years has been especially spectacular in the gray area of nontariff barriers—orderly marketing agreements and other "voluntary" bilateral export restraints as well as unilateral measures by beleaguered governments. It is estimated that in 1981 curbs allowed under GATT rules prevented only $2.5 billion in trade,[3] but measures illegal under GATT rules suppressed more than $50 billion of potential trade.

Finally, some governments favor bilateralism in order to limit trade deficits country by country; the effect is to lower the multilateral benefits of trade, leading to suboptimal allocations of scarce resources. Other governments encourage countertrade, which is estimated to account for more than one-fifth of world trade; countertrade agreements cover compensation or buybacks (technology and pipes for gas), counterpurchases in which the goods traded are unrelated (planes for gas), and barter (trade without the use of money).

The dangers of the rise in protectionism will become fully apparent in the next chapter.

Attitudes and institutions developed during the period of uninterrupted high levels of employment and real economic growth adapted slowly to the entirely different circumstances of the 1970s. While slow economic growth made structural adjustment more difficult, on the whole industrial countries and their populations, especially in Europe, have resisted adjusting.

The problems brought by the refusal to make the necessary structural adjustments have been compounded by the rapid growth of the public sector and social programs that had adverse effects on incentives to work, save, and invest, especially in Europe. Furthermore, in some cases, governments have made direct attempts to avoid the social consequences of structural change by preserving given production and employment structures. Such attempts have aggravated economic inefficiencies and government deficits, crowded the private sector out of the capital markets, stifled the innovative part of the private sector, stopped job creation in new industries and services, and further worsened unemployment.

Monetary policy was given the primary role in controlling the evolution of aggregate demand. The growth of the government sector, which created that demand, was deemed "uncontrollable." The resulting reduction in nominal demand with continuing inflation led to a reduction in output growth.

The fundamental question facing the industrial countries in the 1980s is not the optimal policy mix or the most desirable level of real interest rates, but whether the peoples of the industrial world will accept or continue to refuse to adjust to an environment of slower real growth. To restore a faster trend rate of real growth, large structural changes are necessary. The industrial countries will have to decide soon whether they will implement them or continue to resist them.

For the time being, the collective refusal to implement the necessary structural changes, especially in Europe, is slowing the process of resource transfers needed to adjust to new patterns of comparative advantage arising from such factors as technological change, shifts in demand, and the emergence of new competitors in the world economy.

6

Economic Forces and Institutions in the 1930s and 1980s

The Great Stagnation of the 1970s and early 1980s originated in a structural crisis in the industrialized nations. The growth rates of productivity and investment fell; transfers, subsidies, and government spending rose. Growth slowed in the industrialized countries; the growth rate of international trade declined; and the non-oil developing countries resorted to international borrowing to finance their economies. Finally, in 1982–1983 many developing countries stopped servicing their external debt.

This chapter discusses the causes of the Great Stagnation by distinguishing, for pedagogical reasons, between several crises that are obviously dynamically linked. The macroeconomic crisis in the early 1980s was not one but two crises: the structural crisis that began in the 1970s compounded by the disinflationary crisis of 1980–1982. These two crises will not necessarily lead to a new depression; it is important in this respect to understand that the two crises and the possible depression have different causes.

First, the structural crisis that appeared in the 1970s in the United States and Europe, marked by the return of real economic growth to its secular trend, had three well-defined causes (huge changes in relative energy prices in late 1973 and 1979–1980 forcing large transfers of resources across borders, new sources of supply for foodstuffs and especially manufactures, and technological change), and a less well-defined cause (a general weakening of incentives to work, save, and especially invest). This structural crisis will not be overcome easily even if the relative prices of energy fall further in 1984 and 1985. Long-term policies of adjustment are necessary if the industrialized world wants to escape its secular trend rate of economic growth of 2.5 to 3 percent per year for another short spell of a decade or two.

Second, the disinflationary crisis of 1980–1982 was a reduction in real world economic growth due to the restrictive monetary policy followed by the United States from October 1979 to mid-1982.[1] The effects of this necessary policy of adjustment can very easily be undone.

Third, a new Great Depression could be caused by a trade war that would reduce the level of exports by the non-oil developing countries and hence limit their ability—or make it impossible—to service their debt. This could lead to a collapse of the international banking system and the international economy.

THE MODERN STRUCTURAL CRISIS

In the 1950s and 1960s, the industrial countries experienced an economic growth rate unparalleled in history. In the OECD area, the rate reached 5 percent on average every year from 1961 to 1973. Real private final-consumption expenditure per capita in the OECD area increased by almost 4 percent every year in the same period. This was made possible by two temporary conditions. Throughout the 1950s and 1960s, the relative price of energy with respect to other commodities was very low and falling, while as a group, the industrial countries enjoyed an economic rent on their sales of manufactures due to the absence of competition from the rest of the world. But even at that time things were changing. The average annual rate of GDP growth of the major exporters of manufactures among the non-oil developing countries reached 8.1 percent in 1968–1972. The real GDP of Japan (an exception among industrial countries) was growing at the fantastic average rate of growth of 10 percent per year over the period 1961–1973. Most of these countries started from a very low base.

Following the first oil shock, the relative price of oil was corrected to an equilibrium level that made the development of alternative energy sources economically feasible. Meanwhile the major exporters of manufactures among the developing countries were still catching up; their average annual rate of growth was about 6 percent in 1973–1980. Since these countries were not burdened with high social benefits, the prices of their goods were very competitive on world markets. While the volume of exports of the seven major industrial countries increased by 7 percent per year on average in 1976–1980, it rose by 11 percent per year for the major exporters of manufactures among the developing countries during that same period. These new suppliers overwhelmed traditional industries in Europe and the United States. Since trade unions were powerful in these industries, subsidies increased and discreet or not-so-discreet protectionist measures proliferated.

Hence, after the first oil shock, the combination of changed relative energy prices and new sources of supply weakened the traditional industries of North America and Europe, while through transfers and subsidies, every attempt was made, especially in Europe, to resist the changes brought by the new economic order. These difficulties were compounded by technological change (industrial electronics and robotics) and managerial innovations, but the response of the industrial countries to these changes has been diverse. While Japan has used and is implementing all available new processes of production, North America and Europe have been slow to adapt.

Beyond these three well-defined causes (changes in relative energy prices, new sources of supply, technological change), the structural crisis in North America and Europe has a less well-defined cause—a general weakening of incentives to work, save, and especially invest. The social attitudes and institutions developed during the period of uninterrupted high levels of real economic growth and employment adapted slowly, too slowly, to the entirely different circumstances of the 1970s. The growth of social entitlements was explosive and concentrated on some vocal and well-organized groups. In order to reduce the share of transfers and subsidies in the total output of goods and services, it would have been necessary to cut the social benefits of these groups drastically. Since the costs of these benefits were spread over the entire society, opposition to the benefits was sporadic and ill-organized.

Since the crisis was believed to be (or falsely presented as) temporary in the industrial democracies, political leaders were eager to please these well-organized lobbies. The share of transfers and subsidies reached 20 percent of GDP in Europe (average of Germany, France, the United Kingdom, and Italy) in 1980, and 11.5 percent in the United States and Japan (an increase of a third for the Europeans and almost a doubling for the other two countries over the previous fifteen years).

Beyond these four causes, the structural crisis was deepened by the consequences of decisionmaking under conditions of increasing uncertainty. Large and growing government deficits led to high inflationary expectations, while the accommodation of the deficits by monetary policy in the 1970s led to actual inflation. Large debtors on the international scene, whether governments or corporations, had to be rescued from bankruptcy in 1981–1982. Governments implemented protectionist measures to limit imports; their only effect was to reduce the benefits of international trade. Consequently, the likelihood of large shocks to the international economy rose considerably in the early 1980s. The resulting increase in uncertainty led to a shift from productive to protective investments, while the discrepancy between expected and actual prices (including interest rates) caused what appeared only after the fact as a misallocation of resources.

Reductions in productivity and investment were the channels by which these causes led to reduced growth. Until strong adjustment measures are taken, the consequences of this structural crisis will prevent a return to the growth rates of the 1960s, and any attempt to increase aggregate demand will only lead to a resumption of inflation—even if relative energy prices are somewhat reduced in the next few years beyond the decrease at the beginning of 1983. Unless the economies of Europe and North America adjust, they are condemned to wriggle around the reduced trend rate of growth.

The Disinflationary Crisis of 1980–1982

When the second oil shock occurred, a limited adjustment effort was carried out through monetary restriction in order to avoid an inflationary explosion. But despite the rhetoric, no real change in economic management was implemented. The share of tranfers and subsidies in GDP is still growing, while the share of gross private savings captured by the public authorities of the seven major industrial countries trebled from 1979 to 1982 and stayed at that level in 1983 (see Table 5.5). The indexation of wages ensures that the share of the compensation of employees in domestic factor incomes will essentially remain at the levels reached in the early 1980s. Faced with the prospect of an acceleration of inflation, the United States adopted a restrictive monetary policy, which led to a doubling of U.S. short-term real rates of interest from 1.9 percent in 1980 to 4.4 percent in 1982. Real rates of interest remained high throughout 1983. The rise in the level of uncertainty in the early 1980s increased the *ex ante* demand for real money balances at a time when monetary policy became restrictive in order to bring the expansion of aggregate demand under control. This led to a further contraction of real activity.

Even though Germany, for example, adopted a restrictive monetary policy as early as 1979 and the average real short-term and long-term interest rates increased in the seven major industrial countries broadly in line with the evolution in U.S. financial markets, the U.S. dollar was strongly revalued vis-à-vis the currencies of its main trading partners in 1981 and 1982. The explanation of this phenomenon might reside in the increased demand for dollars in the international economy at a time of reduced supply (see Chapter 4). The effect of this phenomenon was to increase the burden of debt service for the non-oil developing countries since their debt is denominated mostly in U.S. dollars. At a time of rapidly falling industrial production in the United States and elsewhere, there was a succession of debt crises in 1982.

U.S. industrial production, which increased by 2.6 percent from 1980 to 1981, fell by almost 8 percent in 1982. GNP was reduced by almost 2 percent in that same year. Meanwhile, the growth rate of exports of the non-oil developing countries fell from more than 6 percent in 1981 to less than 1 percent in 1982. The total outstanding debt of the non-oil developing countries reached about $610 billion in 1982, and the ratio of the external debt of these countries to their exports of goods and services increased from around 125 percent in 1981 to about 143 percent in 1982. Debt-service payments of the non-oil developing countries quadrupled from 1976 to 1982, reaching almost $110 billion in 1982 or about 24 percent of total exports of goods and services.[2] This ratio stood at a staggering 54 percent for the developing countries of the Americas: Mexico, Argentina, and Brazil almost defaulted simultaneously on their debt obligations in the second half of 1982.

This chain of events was similar to the one that precipitated the Great Depression in the 1930s. Why then did the world economy not collapse in the second half of 1982? First, while the increase in the *ex ante* demand for real money balances was not satisfied until mid-1982 in order to check inflation, the U.S. Federal Reserve decided to accommodate part of this increased demand in the second half of 1982 and first half of 1983: U.S. money stocks started to increase much faster than in the previous two years. This policy was in marked contrast to the one pursued in 1930–1933. Second, a rescheduling of South American debt obligations and timely loans by the IMF enabled world financial authorities to manage the debt crisis; this response was also in marked contrast to the ineptitude of the 1930s. The effort to stave off the world debt crisis involved multilateral debt renegotiations during 1982 and the first ten months of 1983 with 27 countries, or about twice the number involved during the preceding four years. These negotiations were generally conditional on adjustment programs designed by national authorities with the help of the IMF.

Two questions spring to mind: Was the disinflationary crisis necessary and could such a near simultaneous default by major debtors at some point in the next few years degenerate into a new Great Depression?

The answer to the first question is straightforward: the policies of monetary restraint followed since 1979 that led to the global recession of 1980–1982 did not cause the present economic difficulties but merely exposed the underlying weaknesses of the international economic situation, such as the failure to adjust to new patterns of comparative advantage and continued high budget deficits in North America and Europe and overborrowing by developing countries for purposes other than profitable investment. Sending the economy into a recession to check some of these misguided practices was a costly way to start the process of adjustment, but the recession was simply a poor substitute for political leadership (reduction of government subsidies and better coordination of monetary policies in the industrial countries would have limited the disinflationary crisis).

The next section considers the second question.

Is a New Great Depression Possible?

As a depression unfolds, structures are altered and institutions collapse. If we conclude that the structures and institutions of the 1980s are less likely to lead to a depression, this conclusion would apply only as long as the depression had not begun. In other words, the most reassuring conclusion attainable is that the institutions and structures of the 1980s make prevention of depressions relatively easier than did those operating in the 1930s.

Moreover, the United States, as the largest economic power and the ultimate regulator of the world quantity of money, still has the capacity to determine, by and large, the evolution of the international economy. In the 1980s as in the 1930s, a depression would have to engulf the United States to be international. Hence attention in this section focuses on the U.S. economy, but most of its conclusions concerning changes in U.S. structures and institutions apply to Western Europe and Japan.

Economic Structures.   Production and employment are less sensitive to changes in economic activity in the 1980s compared with the late 1920s due to the greater importance of the service sector. The service sector is much less sensitive to business cycles than are other sectors of the economy. The share of the service industry in civilian employment increased almost by half from 1929 to 1980.[3]

On the other hand, the share of international trade in the economies of the industrial countries also increased markedly from 1929 to 1980. The ratio of exports of goods and services to GNP in the United States increased from 6.8 percent in 1929 to 12.5 percent in 1981 (the share of exports of goods and nonfactor services in GDP was smaller; see Table 4.14). Table 4.14 illustrates the importance of the foreign sector in the economies of the industrial countries. Since exports depend on foreign demand, a collapse of the international economy would seriously affect the internationally traded–goods sector of the industrial countries, much more than in the 1930s. The industrial countries are also much more sensitive today to the competition of the major exporters of manufactures among the non-oil developing countries as well as to competition among themselves than they were even ten years ago.

Both the late 1920s and early 1980s were marked by structural rigidities and uncompetitive sectors of the economy: the U.S. farm sector in the 1920s; the steel, auto, and, more generally, traditional U.S. industries in the early 1980s. In the 1920s, economic activity was shifting from farming to industry; in the 1970s and early 1980s from industry to services.

In summary, in nature and magnitude, the structural adjustment problems of the 1920s were no worse than those of the 1980s. And if fluctuations of economic activity are now limited by the size of the service sector, they depend largely on a very unstable foreign sector. In the area of structures, we are really no better off in the 1980s.

National Institutions and Arrangements.   Automatic stabilizers, such as the tax system, are now built into the economic system. Unemployment benefits and social transfers limit the sizable variations in income that were the mark of the interwar period. Unfortunately, they also contribute to increasing government deficits whose financing has negative effects on economic activity.

In the 1920s, farmers were overrepresented in the political system. In the early 1980s, according to all studies of the U.S. electorate, the elderly and government employees vote in much higher proportions than do the other classes of society. These groups do not favor the types of cuts in public spending that could help restore the competitiveness of the economy.

The federal insurance of deposits is potentially the most important difference in financial matters between the 1930s and 1980s. While it introduced an element of stability in the economic system by reducing the risk of runs on banks and hence of a large disintermediation comparable to that of 1931–1933, it also led depositors to ignore the consequences of suboptimal bank lending. Since deposits are insured against the possible bankruptcy of financial institutions, depositors have no incentive to verify the financial soundness of bank portfolios.[4] This could explain why there were no checks on bank overlending to poorly managed corporations or to developing countries for motives other than profitable investment at a time of high demand for credit in 1974–1982.[5]

Hence institutions and arrangements designed to improve the stability and efficiency of the economic system have led to some perverse consequences that are or could be destabilizing.

International Institutions and Arrangements.   The noticeable international institutional change between the early 1930s and the 1980s is in the exchange rate regime. Gold parities were maintained beyond reason in the United States and France in the face of large capital movements in the early 1930s, but the international monetary system is much more flexible now. On the other hand, the sheer amount of capital movements in the 1980s makes it difficult for national authorities trying to implement a rational economic program to resist the under- and overshootings of exchange rate equilibria that are the mark of flexible exchange rates.

In the 1930s, Central Europe was heavily dependent on U.S. and British loans, but even the British banking system was not as exposed to the risk of German default on its foreign obligations as the international banking system is today exposed to the risk of default of the non-oil developing countries. Still, when the German default came, it brought down sterling and the international financial system with it.

In another area of international institutions, the GATT seems unable to control informal trade curbs covering gentlemen's agreements, price monitoring, "export forecasting," or obvious quotas.

One international institution that functions well is the IMF, which certainly did an excellent job in staving off the South American debt crises. But the financial means of the IMF may be too limited in relation to the problems.

Business Cycles. Two items in the present economic situation compare unfavorably with that of the late 1920s. While the U.S. economy was growing strongly in 1925–1928, U.S. national output in 1983 will barely surpass its 1979 level. The administrative budgets of the federal government showed a surplus each year from 1920 to 1930, but the federal deficit is reaching unprecedented levels in the 1980s, and government borrowing is burdening the demand on U.S. and indirectly world financial markets, keeping real interest rates high.

The next item is positive. Real stocks of money in the United States were constant in 1928–1929, while real M1 declined and real M2 was stable in 1980–1981. When problems developed, the Federal Reserve System proved it was much more flexible than in the 1930s by accommodating the increased *ex ante* demand for real money balances after mid-1982.

The prospects for economic recovery in the United States and elsewhere point to slow growth after 1984, which could lead to renewed calls for increased protectionism.

The external debt of non-oil developing countries will continue to grow, albeit at slower rates than in the past few years. For the next few years, debt-service ratios, such as debt payments as a percentage of exports, will remain high (see Appendix A).

Overall, comparing structures, institutions, and business cycles, the international economy does not appear much more stable or sound in 1980–1983 than it was in 1925–1928. Should a trade war develop and limit the exports of developing countries, debt ratios would reach unmanageable levels (see Table A.3 in Appendix A for an illustration), and world financial institutions might not be able to avoid a massive and simultaneous default on international debt obligations. This could lead to a collapse of the international banking system and of the international economy, possibly provoking unprecedented movements of disintermediation in the various domestic financial markets. A new and devastating Great Depression would ensue.

Conclusions

To take the comparison of the 1930s and 1980s a step further, the Great Depression can also be analyzed in terms of two crises that did not have to lead to a depression. First, the structural crisis of the 1920s was less severe than its counterpart in the 1970s. Also marked by new sources of supply of foodstuffs and manufactures as well as by technological change, the economy of the 1920s experienced changes in relative energy prices that were smaller than those of the 1970s and did not entail large transfers of resources across borders (although reparations payments occasioned transfers of resources across borders, they did not reach the scale of those in the 1970s and early 1980s). In addition, incentives to work, save, and especially invest were not diminished in the United States in the 1920s. On the contrary, profits increased strongly, unemployment was low, government spending was stable, and the budget showed a surplus.

Second, the restrictive monetary policy followed in the United States in 1928–1929 broke the upward phase of the 1928 business cycle during the winter of 1929–1930, but these negative effects could have been overcome by increasing liquidity, with no risk of inflation since prices had been stable or declining for several years.

Indeed, without policy mistakes in monetary and international trade matters, the Great Depression would not have occurred. The main lesson of the 1930s for the 1980s is that should mistakes of a similar nature be made, a new Great Depression could set in.

In the environment that must be re-created to allow a balanced growth of the international economy, the role of monetary policy is to maintain the stability of the financial and price systems. An adequate supply of money accommodating increases in real activity in a progressive manner would avoid the collapse of the 1930s as well as the volatility of the early 1970s, the major factors in the Great Depression and the Great Recession.

At a time of disinflation, in the transition from one steady state to a more favorable one, monetary authorities must allow the economy sufficient time to adapt. A policy of disinflation must be strict at first in order to break inflationary expectations, but in the last stages of disinflation it might be necessary to pump some liquidity into the financial system.[6]

The decline in nominal interest rates in the second half of 1982, if maintained, will help reduce the costs of servicing the large external debt of the developing countries, and the extensive reschedulings of government and bank debt in the early 1980s have avoided potentially hazardous defaults. But the debts are still large and increasing, and they will have to be repaid. Indeed, should debt-service obligations continue to be rescheduled on a large scale in 1984–1985 the bunching of debt repayment obligations in 1986–1990 could be unbearable at the aggregate level. The severe testing of international financial statesmanship during the winter 1982–1983, which ended so well thanks to excellent decisionmaking by the IMF, Federal Reserve System, and BIS, might be only a foretaste of what to expect in the second half of the 1980s.

Price (including interest and exchange rate) uncertainties have marked decisionmaking in the international economy since the abandonment of fixed exchange rates in the first half of 1973, before the oil shock.[7] To maintain grossly under- or overvalued exchange rates, as in the 1930s, is a source of imbalances that can be destructive, but letting exchange rates float freely is not a superior regime. International cooperation will be needed to stabilize exchange rate movements.

International free trade brings the benefits associated with specialization in the comparative advantage of each country (see Appendix B). Coupled with a strengthening of the multilateral principle of free trade, determined national policies to increase incentives to work, save, and invest and to reduce the level of transfers and subsidies will create the conditions for a return to prosperity.

Three general conclusions follow from this study of the macroeconomic crisis in the 1980s with the benefit of the experience gained from the Great Depression.

First, there is a need for pervasive adjustment. Developing countries must reduce their current-account imbalances until the last cent of deficit can be justified as an investment for the future. Developed countries must reduce their government deficits and cut the amount of transfers and subsidies until the last cent of expenditure can be shown to increase productive capacity and further social and intellectual progress with the effect of increasing the quality of the human capital stock of society.

Second, the development needs of the non-oil-producing countries are such that there is scope for a Marshall Plan for the Third World. Transfers of long-term capital for profitable investment, of technical knowledge, and of managerial skills are a necessity; these transfers are *not* inflationary. The United States, as the ultimate source of dollars, must again take the lead in this effort. Japan should contribute this time since it stands to gain the most from the initiative. Imports by the developing world would spur activity in the industrial countries, while increased exports by the Third World would help it repay its debts.

Third, the good times are over. Everywhere, incentives to work, save, invest, and develop new sources of energy must be increased. Incentives and expectations to be "transferred" and "subsidized" out of problems must be eliminated.

Three conditions are necessary for future growth:

1. Protectionism cannot be allowed to develop;
2. The international banking system must be reformed (see Appendix C);
3. The monetary policies of the major industrial countries must be coordinated.

The Great Depression did not have to happen, and the policy mistakes that made it inevitable must not be repeated. Much courage and vision will be needed to lead the world safely through the 1980s.

APPENDIXES

A

Alternative Scenarios for 1984–1986

The IMF developed, in its *1982 World Economic Outlook*, three scenarios to illustrate the possible consequences of alternative policies. The IMF implicitly assumes that throughout the period under study structures and institutions will not be altered and that the trade restrictiveness of the industrial countries toward the exports of the non-oil developing countries will be unchanged from 1982 to 1986.

The scenarios presented here were revised in 1983, but according to the IMF (*1983 World Economic Outlook*, p. 15), "the broad results are essentially unchanged." The IMF published only the results for scenario A (see below) in the *1983 World Economic Outlook*. I used these published results to update the 1982 scenarios.

Scenario A is based on the assumption that industrial countries will persist with policies of monetary restraint reinforced by compatible and supportive fiscal policies and by a certain effort to reform rigid structures in labor and goods markets. In scenario A, the average annual rate of growth of the industrial countries would reach 3 percent in 1984–1986, and inflation would be cut to 5 percent by 1986. Unemployment would be essentially unchanged from 1983 to 1986.

Scenario B assumes a relaxation of monetary restraint at a time of rising unemployment as well as a failure to develop supportive fiscal policies and structural reforms. In scenario B, economic growth in the industrial countries would be reduced to 2 percent per year in 1984–1986, inflation would rise to 8.5 percent by 1986, and unemployment would increase further from 1983 to 1986.

Scenario C assumes the same monetary and fiscal policies as scenario A. It also assumes that major structural reforms are implemented to deal with rigidities in goods and labor markets and that the response of economic agents to those measures is positive. Real growth reaches 4.5 percent in 1984–1986, and inflation falls to around 4 percent by 1986.

The interesting aspect of the IMF work is that it shows what would happen under these alternative scenarios to the non-oil developing countries (using computerized economic models and detailed information on all the countries).

The crucial assumption concerning the developing world is that the countries confronted with serious external imbalances will implement comprehensive programs of adjustment (fiscal and monetary reforms will lead to slower increases of the monetary aggregates, realistic exchange rates combined with changes in domestic prices will reflect world market prices, government controls and regulations will be attenuated, and interest rates will be allowed to reflect real rates of return). If scenario B prevails, the adjustment programs will be more severe than under A or C.

In its results, the IMF compares estimated data for 1982 with expected data for 1986. Changes between these two years are essentially gradual. The results are expressed in terms of current-account balances and debt-service ratios. The crucial implicit assumption is that all the individual countries maintain their access to capital markets, or, in other words, that the current-account deficits do get financed throughout the period.

Table A.1 presents medium-term projections of payments balances on current account, while Table A.2 projects the debt burden. (A, B, and C refer to the scenarios.)

In Table A.2, the non-oil developing countries are further divided between net-oil exporters (Bahrain, Bolivia, Congo, Ecuador, Egypt, Gabon, Malaysia, Mexico, Peru, Syria, Trinidad and Tobago, and Tunisia) and the others.

Table A.1 shows that under scenario B prospects will not improve for the developing world in the 1980s; the current-account deficit as a percentage of exports of goods and services will deteriorate from 19 percent in 1982 to 20 percent in 1986. Table A.2 shows that under scenario B, debt ratios will essentially be unchanged from 1982 to 1986.

Implicit in these scenarios is that in 1984–1986 the average annual rate of growth of the volume of exports of goods will reach more or less (depending on the scenario) 5 percent for the net-oil exporters and 6 percent for the net-oil importers. Is this realistic? Indeed, one should contemplate three possibilities:

First, in scenario B1, the United States uses all its economic, diplomatic, and even strategic powers to maintain the existing international economic system, with protectionism increasing mildly and discreetly. No major debtors are allowed to default, and the international banking system meets the

TABLE A.1　MEDIUM-TERM PROJECTIONS OF
　　　　　　PAYMENTS BALANCES ON CURRENT ACCOUNT
　　　　　　NON-OIL DEVELOPING COUNTRIES, 1982–1986

		1986		
	1982	A	B	C
In billions of dollars	− 87	− 93	− 130	− 70
As percentage of exports of goods and services	− 19	− 14	− 20	− 10

SOURCES: IMF, *World Economic Outlook* (Washington, D.C., 1982 and 1983); and author's adjustments.

TABLE A.2　MEDIUM-TERM PROJECTIONS OF DEBT BURDEN
　　　　　　NON-OIL DEVELOPING COUNTRIES, 1982–1986
　　　　　　(PERCENTAGE)

		1986		
	1982	A	B	C
Net oil exporters				
Debt ratio[a]	139	155	165	140
Debt-service ratio[b]	32	30	36	28
Net oil importers				
Debt ratio[a]	107	102	115	90
Debt-service ratio[b]	18	16	18	14

SOURCES: IMF, *World Economic Outlook* (Washington, D.C., 1982 and 1983); and author's adjustments.
[a]Ratio of year-end long-term debt to exports of goods and services.
[b]Payments (interest and amortization) as percentage of exports of goods and services.

financing needs of the developing countries. The situation deteriorates only slightly compared with scenario B.

Second, in scenario B2, the United States lets the other industrial countries increase barriers to trade, adapts to the modified world, and pumps enough dollars into the international financial system to avoid a collapse. The debt-service ratios of the developing world increase markedly.

Third, in scenario B3, the United States initiates an open trade war sometime in 1984 or 1985, as it did in June 1930 with the Hawley-Smoot

TABLE A.3   MEDIUM-TERM PROJECTIONS OF
             DEBT BURDEN WITH TRADE WAR
             NON-OIL DEVELOPING COUNTRIES, 1982–1986
             (PERCENTAGE)

		1986		
	1982	*B1*	*B2*	*B3*
Net oil exporters				
Debt ratio	139	175	210	330
Debt-service ratio	32	38	46	72
Net oil importers				
Debt ratio	107	120	150	230
Debt-service ratio	18	19	23	36

SOURCE: Author's estimates (see text).

NOTE: See Table A.2 for definitions; this table assumes the amounts of debt in 1986 given in scenario B and different levels of exports of goods and services. Obviously this implies that further drastic adjustments are implemented to limit the current-account deficits. This naturally entails a reduction in the exports of the rest of the world to the developing nations.

Tariff. The debt-service ratios of the developing world become unmanageable; they are given only to show what they would be if they could be financed. If they cannot be financed, most major debtors default, and the international banking system collapses. The volume of world trade falls by a third; the United States pumps enough dollars into the system to avoid a deflation, but the value of the exports of goods and services of the non-oil developing countries is cut in half by 1986 (due to an adverse evolution in the terms of trade). A new Great Depression sets in for most of the 1980s.

Table A.3 presents medium-term indicative projections of debt burden for non-oil developing countries under alternative assumptions in the level of protectionism. Given present trends in international borrowing, debt-service ratios will not be markedly different through the end of the 1980s from those shown in Table A.2. Hence, the impact of a trade war initiated during the 1980s would essentially be similar to what is shown in Table A.3.

B

Benefits of Free Trade

The arguments for free trade are familiar, but they bear repeating. (For a good, mathematical exposition, see Elhanan Helpman and Assaf Razin, *A Theory of International Trade Under Uncertainty* [New York: Academic Press, 1978].)

Consider two countries, one that produces only food and one that produces only clothing. If the first country produces more food than it needs, it disposes of the surplus by exchanging it for clothing. But even if it produces less food than it needs, it is ready to exchange part of this food (provided that there is enough left to survive) for some clothing. It is apparent that it will be ready to sell food for clothing as long as it gains more satisfaction from the clothing acquired than it loses by disposing of the food.

Likewise the second country is ready to exchange clothing for food. Each country is trying to get as much as possible of the other country's commodity in exchange for as little as possible of its own production. Both countries will finally agree on an equilibrium price at which they are both ready to trade so much food for so much clothing. This will be the relative price of one commodity for the other. The ratio of exchange of x units of food for y units of clothing expresses the terms of the exchange or terms of trade. By increasing each country's level of satisfaction, trade makes both countries better off since it allows both nations to consume food *and* clothing.

Each country's endowments will determine the commodity that it produces. If the first country has only fertile plains while the other possesses a well-trained work force and a large quantity of industrial capital but has no plains, each will naturally specialize in producing food or clothing, respectively.

One can go a step further and assume that the first country has plains that are relatively more fertile than the second one, while the second country has a relatively better trained work force and relatively more efficient or productive or modern industrial capital stock than the first one. Then the first country is said to have a *relative* or *comparative advantage* in producing food, and the second one a comparative advantage in producing clothing. Both countries will be better off in specializing in their respective areas of comparative advantage and exchanging their output for the other country's production since this will increase the collective efficiency by combining the scarce resources of both countries taken together. This will increase, in other words, the maximum attainable output or potential output for a given amount of scarce resources. By reaping the benefits of specialization in the comparative advantage of each country, international trade increases both the welfare of each trading nation and world output.

When the patterns of comparative advantage change through time and across borders, each country must combine its scarce resources in new ways in order to benefit from its new comparative advantage; by continuing to combine its scarce resources in the most efficient manner, each country remains competitive, maximizes its production, and contributes to increasing world output. On the other hand, if a country refuses to adapt to its new comparative advantage or if it wastes scarce resources, it reduces its potential output as well as the overall level of productive efficiency in the world economy; hence it reduces world output while losing its competitiveness. A sustained loss of competitiveness will prove economically unbearable, and the country will be forced to adjust to the changed economic order. In the meantime, and if enough countries refuse to adjust, the growth or even the level of world output can decline, entailing unpopular reductions in world consumption.

But even if changes in patterns of comparative advantage and international division of labor are ultimately irresistible, are they generally desirable?

Endowments of land and population determine initially and through their evolution the patterns of comparative advantage between countries. By accumulating human skills and physical capital, nations can modify their comparative advantage; they can increase it by hard and intelligent work, by saving, and by investing part of their production. Nations can also reduce their comparative advantage by wasting scarce resources or by reducing incentives to work, save, and invest. Changes in comparative advantage due to increased rates of accumulation of human skills and physical capital as well as improvements in the productive efficiency of some nations are positive if the expanded accumulation and efficiency are obtained through increased incentives to work, save, and invest; they are negative if the growth of accumulation and efficiency is secured in ways that corrupt human values or humble free men. Positive changes in comparative advantage are desirable since they increase the world stocks of scarce resources and the average world level of productive efficiency. Therefore they increase world output, consumption, and welfare.

In the 1960s, 1970s, and early 1980s, Japan and many countries in the developing world increased their rates of accumulation of human and physical capital stocks and improved their productive efficiency to the benefit of the international community. At the same time, however, the other industrial countries decreased incentives to work, save, and invest and wasted scarce resources through extravagant transfers and subsidies and destructive budget deficits. The patterns of comparative advantage naturally shifted in favor of the first group of countries. By refusing to adapt to these changes of comparative advantage, the latter countries further reduced the world's productive efficiency and hence the rate of growth of world output.

By bringing the benefits associated with specialization in the comparative advantage of each country, international free trade is the only bounty left in a world of scarcity. Hence nations and groups of nations must reassert the multilateral principle of free trade. Further, since a trade war would cause a collapse of the international economy, nations can only lose much for trying to achieve petty advantages. Indeed, if a nation dislikes some of the effects of the new patterns of comparative advantage, it can alter its system of incentives to work, save, and invest and eliminate the waste of scarce resources: this is the only rational way out of the macroeconomic crisis experienced in some industrial countries.

C

International Lending and the International Financial System

INTERNATIONAL COOPERATION OF LENDERS OF LAST RESORT AND OF BANK SUPERVISORS

International banking expanded at a rapid pace in the 1960s and especially the 1970s. Bank financing contributed to the exceptional growth in international trade; many banks started or greatly expanded their operations in foreign countries and played a major role in the "recycling" of oil money, lending heavily to developing countries. While the activities of banks became more internationalized, bank supervision and regulation remained largely domestically oriented.

After March 1973, floating exchange rates encouraged some foreign exchange speculation. The Bankhaus I. D. Herstatt of Cologne and the Franklin National Bank of New York were spectacular losers at the new game, and they were both forced to close their doors in June 1974, following unauthorized foreign exchange speculation by employees. Herstatt was closed permanently, and Franklin was merged with another bank. The respective central banks covered all domestic and foreign liabilities. This episode appeared to create a precedent, and it was thought that central banks would henceforth be responsible for banks under their jurisdiction.

In September 1974, the BIS announced the creation of a Committee on Banking Regulations and Supervisory Practices (present membership includes the Group of Ten major industrialized countries, Switzerland, and Luxembourg) in order to improve the coordination and the quality of the surveillance exercised by national authorities over the international banking system. This committee is called the Basel or the Cooke Committee (after Peter Cooke of the Bank of England, its chairman since 1977). The Basel Committee is best known for the concordat on international supervisory cooperation, or the Basel Concordat, endorsed by the BIS governors in

December 1975. The concordat specifies the responsibilities of national supervisory authorities in international banking but deals only with bank supervision and not with lender of last resort operations.

The collapse of Banco Ambrosiano, Italy's largest private bank, in 1982 strongly affected the world of supervision. On July 12, Midland Bank of Great Britain declared default on a loan of $40 million when it did not receive payments of interest and principal from BAH, a Luxembourg-based holding company controlled by Banco Ambrosiano. Loans totaling more than half a billion dollars owed to more than 250 banks were declared in default as a result of the action of Midland. The Bank of Italy argued that BAH was a financial holding company and not a bank, and therefore the Italian authorities said that they should not be involved in averting the collapse or assist in the liquidation of BAH.

Following this incident, a revised Basel Concordat was published on June 9, 1983. The new concordat stresses that "banking supervisory authorities cannot be fully satisfied about the soundness of individual banks unless they can examine the totality of each bank's business worldwide through the technique of consolidation." It further states that

> effective cooperation between host and parent authorities is a central prerequisite for the supervision of banks' international operations. In relation to the supervision of banks' foreign establishments there are two basic principles which are fundamental to such cooperation and which call for consultation and contacts between respective host and parent authorities: firstly, that no foreign banking establishment should escape supervision; and secondly, that the supervision should be adequate. In giving effect to these principles, host authorities should ensure that parent authorities are informed immediately of any serious problems which arise in a parent bank's foreign establishment. Similarly, parent authorities should inform host authorities when problems arise in a parent bank which are likely to affect the parent bank's foreign establishment.

In spite of the better definition of supervisory responsibilities between national authorities included in the new concordat, guidelines concerning solvency and liquidity ratios and the making of provisions remain imprecise in some countries and internationally. More significantly, many of the 100 banks, among the 500 largest commercial banks, that are headquartered outside of the OECD are improperly supervised. Some international banks in offshore centers are not supervised at all.

Moreover, the responsibilities of central banks as lenders of last resort are not well divided. In the Basel Communiqué of September 1974 (which should not be mistaken with the Basel Concordat), the BIS governors declared:

> The [governors] recognized that it would not be practical to lay down in advance detailed rules and procedures for the provision of temporary liquidity. But they were satisfied that means are available for that purpose and will be used if and when necessary.

No further details are officially known. As the Italian authorities' refusal to cover the foreign liabilities of the Banco Ambrosiano made apparent, the definition and the sharing of responsibilities are not always clear. Many studies on the subject even express doubts about the real substance of the agreement, and there have been calls to publish its contents. On the other hand, it has been argued that in order to avoid reckless behavior, it is not desirable to define and publicize specific rules designed to assist troubled banks. However, with international banks still improperly supervised and responsibilities of lenders of last resort not clearly defined, problems could emerge.

First, some large international banks have lent too much to too few borrowers and could not easily withstand a default from a large debtor. Second, some of these banks are improperly managed. Third, and most important, due to large interbank deposits, the failure of a bank in an unsupervised area could spread to the rest of the world through the panic multiplier.

Some reforms are called for. First, the technical problems of supervision identified above should be solved rapidly. Second, supervision should be enforced on all international banks; this could be achieved by imposing limits or other penalties on interbank deposits and credit lines from banks of countries that accept the Basel Concordat to banks in countries that do not. Third, the responsibilities of lenders of last resort should be defined more clearly, without necessarily being made public. To protect society from moral hazard, it should be made clear that banks that are insolvent as a result of fraud will be allowed to fail.

At present, commercial bank lending is contracting at a time when the borrowing needs of the developing countries are increasing; multilateral lending must counter sudden reductions in international lending.

Multilateral Lending

The obligations of countries that experience debt-servicing difficulties can be rescheduled. Reschedulings of obligations on debt owed to or guaranteed by the government or the official agencies of the participating creditor countries are usually (although not necessarily) organized by the Paris Club; normally, 85 to 95 percent of both principal and interest obligations on medium- and long-term debt, including arrears, due during the consolidation period, are rescheduled over seven to nine years with a grace period of three to four years. Debt-service obligations to commercial banks are usually rescheduled following negotiations between a steering committee representing the banks and the debtor country; normally between 80 and 100 percent of principal obligations, including arrears on principal obligations, due during the consolidation period, are rescheduled over seven to eight years with a grace period of two to three years. Although reschedulings provide temporary breathing space at a cost, the loans must be repaid and new sources of financing must still be found.

Multilateral financing to developing countries is provided by international institutions. The IMF provides short- to medium-term financing for balance-of-payments deficits, at a cost: a set of rules or "conditionality" defines the adjustment required from a country that wishes to borrow from the IMF. The World Bank and other development banks provide long-term financing for specific projects. Recently the World Bank introduced a program of structural adjustment lending (SAL); various interest rates are charged. The resources of these institutions (in spite of recent improvements) are inadequate to maintain the necessary level of development financing for the non-oil-producing countries.

The need for multilateral lending in this transitional phase of changing private international lending behavior is evident in recent statistics. Net new international lending through commercial banks included in the BIS reporting area fell from $165 billion in 1981 to $95 billion in 1982. Net new lending to the non-oil developing countries was cut in half from $51 billion in 1981 to $25 billion in 1982. Since the financing needs of the non-oil developing countries, as measured by their current-account deficit, fell by about $21 billion from 1981 to 1982 (see Table 4.8), long-term borrowing from official sources, use of IMF credits, and short-term borrowing of monetary authorities from other central banks had to fill the gap in the financing needs of developing countries in 1982. Since net new lending from commercial banks to developing countries is not expected to resume on its pre-1982 scale in the near future, multilateral or official lending will have to compensate for this lack of private funding in order to smooth the adjustment process in developing countries.

RULES FOR FURTHER INTERNATIONAL LENDING

Information and statistics on the flow of funds from commercial banks to recipient countries must be improved. Current initiatives built around the concept of an international banking institute are of great interest. Bimonthly reporting to the BIS of all lending could be enforced on all banks of the BIS area as well as on banks outside the area by setting up a system of penalties on interbank deposits and credit lines from area to non-area banks. The data could be made public within a month of reporting. Although technically difficult to organize, this is feasible.

When this is achieved, an organization, probably the IMF, might be asked to set indicative ceilings on commercial bank lending to countries according to the needs and extent of the adjustment pursued. These ceilings would be set after consultations with all interested parties and would be communicated only to the supervisory authorities. Coupled with the supervisory reforms called for above, these measures would ensure an orderly transfer of resources to developing countries. These measures would be an effective, reasonable, and practical substitute for an international lender of last resort. They would present, in the end, smaller difficulties of implementation than the provision of lender of last resort services involving *a priori* unlimited transfers of currencies across borders, with all the consequences for exchange rates and international capital flows.

Finally, in order to foster new commercial bank lending to developing countries, such lending made in agreement with international guidelines could be partly secured by automatic refinancing agreements with participating central banks and possible cross-default clauses on joint private and multilateral lending.

Notes

CHAPTER I

1. Sidney Ratner, *The Tariff in American History* (New York: Van Nostrand Co., 1972), p. 53.

2. League of Nations, *World Economic Survey* (Geneva, 1932), p. 72.

3. "The Credit Situation in Germany," Report of the committee appointed on the recommendation of the London Conference, 1931, *The Economist* (supplement), August 22, 1931, p. 2.

4. Quarterly data, seasonally adjusted. Source: Harold Barger, *Outlay and Income in the United States, 1921–1938* (New York: NBER, 1942).

5. The book value of manufacturers' inventories, which increased by 6.1 percent in the year ending in the first quarter of 1930, fell by 5.5 percent (annual rate) from the first to the second quarter of 1930.

6. Brian Kantor, "The British Experience in the Interwar Period," Working Paper (Pittsburgh, Pa.: Carnegie-Mellon University, 1979), p. 56.

7. Milton Friedman and Anna Schwartz, *A Monetary History of the United States* (New York: NBER, 1963), p. 317.

8. Ibid., pp. 317–18.

9. This agreement was worked out as part of the package needed to present the devaluation of the franc to the public.

10. Although the record on economic growth and current-account position did not make a small devaluation necessary, the British economy was perceived at the time as much weaker than it really was. The devaluation would have eliminated this false perception.

11. U.S. exports and imports of goods and services: $5.4 and $4.4 billion, respectively, in 1930; world exports of goods in 1930: $26.5 billion.

CHAPTER 2

1. Friedman and Schwartz, *Monetary History*, pp. 313–14.

2. Allan Meltzer, "Monetary and Other Explanations of the Start of the Great Depression," *Journal of Monetary Economics* 2 (1976): 455–71.

3. One can say that the "United Kingdom isolated its economy" from the British point of view. From an international point of view, by devaluing more than was needed to re-establish confidence, the British helped precipitate the world depression.

CHAPTER 3

1. Peter Temin, *Did Monetary Forces Cause the Great Depression?* (New York: Norton, 1976).

2. Thomas Mayer, "Consumption in the Great Depression," *Journal of Political Economy* 86 (1978): 139–45.

3. For harsher dismissals of Temin's argument, see Arthur Gandolfi and James Lothian, "Did Monetary Forces Cause the Great Depression?" *Journal of Money, Credit and Banking* 9 (1977): 679–91; and Anna Schwartz, "Understanding 1929–1933," in Karl Brunner, ed., *The Great Depression Revisited* (Boston: Martinus Nijhoff Publishing, 1981), pp. 5–48.

4. Robert J. Gordon and James A. Wilcox, "Monetary Interpretations of the Great Depression: An Evaluation and Critique," in Brunner, *Great Depression Revisited*, pp. 49–107.

5. Allan H. Meltzer, "Comments on 'Monetary Interpretations of the Great Depression,' " in Brunner, *Great Depression Revisited*, pp. 148–64.

6. Ibid., p. 157.

7. See Don Patinkin, *Money, Interest and Prices*, 2d ed. (New York: Harper & Row, 1965).

8. See Robert J. Barro, "Rational Expectations and the Role of Monetary Policy," *Journal of Monetary Economics* 2 (1976): 1–32; Robert E. Lucas, "Expectations and the Neutrality of Money," *Journal of Economic Theory* 4 (1972): 103–24; idem, "Rules, Discretion, and the Role of the Economic Advisor," in Stanley Fischer, ed., *Rational Expectations and Economic Policy* (Chicago: University of Chicago Press, 1980), pp. 199–210; Thomas J. Sargent, "Rational Expectations, the Real Rate of Interest, and the Natural Rate of Unemployment," *Brookings Papers on Economic Activity* 2 (1973): 429–80; Thomas J. Sargent and Neil Wallace, "Rational Expectations and the Dynamics of Hyperinflation," *International Economic Review* 14 (1973): 328–50; Thomas J. Sargent and Neil Wallace, "Rational Expectations, the Optimal Monetary Instrument, and the Optimal Money Supply Rule," *Journal of Political Economy* 83 (1975): 241–54; and Thomas J.

Sargent and Neil Wallace, "Rational Expectations and the Theory of Economic Policy," *Journal of Monetary Economics* 2 (1976): 169–83.

9. Robert E. Lucas, "Methods and Problems in Business Cycle Theory," Working Paper (Chicago: University of Chicago Press, March 1980), p. 19.

10. John Muth, "Rational Expectations and the Theory of Price Movements," *Econometrica* 29 (1961): 315–35.

11. The *ex ante* demand for real money balances also depends negatively on the opportunity cost of holding real money balances. If from time t_o to time t_1, the level of prices or the rate of inflation falls, the opportunity cost is reduced, increasing the quantity of real money balances demanded.

12. *New York Times*, May 5, 1930.

13. Lars Jonung, *The Depression in Sweden and the United States: A Comparison of Causes and Policies* (Lund, Sweden: University of Lund, 1978), pp. 11–12.

CHAPTER 4

1. The OECD succeeded the Organization for European Economic Cooperation, which had been created in 1948.

2. See OECD, *National Accounts, 1952–1981*, vol. 1 (Paris, 1983). In order to compare data for different countries, it is necessary to convert national accounts data into a common unit of currency. One cannot use exchange rates to establish a true ranking of economic powers, but it is possible to construct national accounts for each country by valuation of goods and services sold in different countries at a common set of average international prices (purchasing power parities). Since the prices used are averages covering all the goods or services produced within the group of countries as a whole, no single country exerts an undue influence on the results. The *numéraire* currency chosen to express the results can be the U.S. dollar; but clearly, the underlying methodology does not assign any special importance to the United States.

3. Except when otherwise indicated, the source of the data given in this section is OECD, *Historical Statistics, 1960–1980* (Paris, 1982).

4. Excess of the value added of resident industries over the sum of their costs of employee compensation, consumption of fixed capital, and indirect taxes reduced by subsidies.

5. Sum of (1) all wages and salaries, in cash and in kind, paid to employees, (2) the contributions made by employers to social security schemes on behalf of their employees, and (3) the contributions, paid or imputed, made by employers to private pension arrangements, family allowances, health insurance, layoff and severance pay, and other casualty insurance, life insurance, and similar schemes on behalf of their employees.

6. For an analysis of the impact of growth in the industrial countries and other factors on the external debt situation of developing countries, see William Cline, *International Debt and the Stability of the World Economy* (Washington, D.C.: Institute for International Economics, 1983).

7. IMF, *World Economic Outlook* (Washington, D.C., 1983), p. 8.

8. Otto Eckstein, *The Great Recession* (New York: North-Holland, 1978), p. 32.

9. Ibid., p. 142.

CHAPTER 5

1. IMF, "Developments in International Trade Policy" (Washington, D.C., November 1982).

2. Ibid., p. 5.

3. The GATT lays down the rules for fair behavior in international trade. It came into force on January 1, 1948, and has been the forum for successive trade liberalization negotiations. The Tokyo Round was launched in 1973 at a GATT ministerial conference; the next such conference was held in Geneva in November 1982.

CHAPTER 6

1. Although I consider that a restrictive U.S. monetary policy will affect the world primarily through interest and exchange rate changes, I was asked "Did the supply of U.S. dollars in fact decline worldwide in the early 1980s? Given the size of the deficit in the U.S. current account in 1982, wasn't the rest of the world acquiring dollars?" The answer is that the cumulative U.S. current-account deficit over the period 1979–1982 was in fact a surplus of $15.6 billion (IMF, *World Economic Outlook*, p. 185).

2. The previous data and ratios refer to total debt, including short-term debt as presented in Table 4.11.

3. The proportion of employees on nonagricultural payrolls was divided as follows: in 1929, 42 percent in the goods-producing sector and 58 percent in the service-producing sector; in 1970, 33 percent in the goods-producing sector and 67 percent in the service-producing sector. At the same time, nonfarm employment as a percentage of civilian employment increased from 77 percent in 1929 to 96 percent in 1970, and employment in services as a percentage of civilian employment reached 66 percent in 1980. (U.S. Department of Commerce, *Historical Statistics of the United States, Colonial Times to 1970* [Washington, D.C.: Government Printing Office, 1975].)

4. Even though there are limits on the amounts insured, in practice all non-bank deposits have been protected. But there was an interesting innovation in U.S. financial practices in 1982: no protection was provided for interbank depositors when a regional bank failed.

5. Although banks were encouraged to "recycle oil money," they were not told to ignore prudent behavior.

6. The Federal Reserve, in sharp contrast to the 1930s, understands today the necessity to accommodate an increased demand for real money balances when uncertainty increases. The Federal Open Market Committee (FOMC) decided at its meeting on October 5, 1982, in what will historically be seen as a momentous action, that it would not set a specific objective for the growth of M1 during the fourth quarter of 1982 and that it would allow M2 to grow above the range for 1982 that the committee had reaffirmed in July. The Federal Reserve continued this liberal policy through the winter of 1982–83.

On July 20, 1983, Paul A. Volcker, chairman of the Federal Reserve Board, commented on the decisions taken by the FOMC during the preceding week; he announced that the growth of M1 at a 14 percent annual rate during the first half of 1983 would not be reversed. His justification was that "NOW accounts [a component of M1], where the growth has been most rapid, are not only transaction balances, but now have a 'savings' or 'liquid asset' component. For a time at least, uncertainty about the financial and economic outlook, and less fear about inflation, may also have bolstered the desire to hold money." As a consequence, "in monitoring M1, the committee felt that an appropriate approach would be to assess future growth from a base of the second quarter of 1983, looking toward growth close to, or below, nominal GNP. Specifically, the range was set at 5 to 9 percent for the remainder of this year, and at 1 percent lower—4 to 8 percent—for 1984." The 1983 target growth range for M2 remained at 7 to 10 percent from its base in February–March 1983.

This analysis of the Federal Reserve falls within the framework outlined in Chapter 3. But there is another reason that leads me to support this analysis. A large international demand for dollars remains unsatisfied; a tightening of U.S. monetary policy to reverse the increase of M1 in the first half of 1983 would put added pressures on an already strained international financial market.

7. Until 1971, the currencies of the member-countries of the IMF were linked by fixed exchange rates. On August 15, 1971, President Nixon announced that the dollar would no longer be convertible in gold, and in the following weeks, most countries had to let their currencies float upward to avoid buying dollars. On December 18, 1971, the dollar was officially devalued and some currencies revalued in the Smithsonian Agreement. On February 12, 1973, the United States devalued the dollar a second time. Then in March 1973, the system of fixed exchange rates was abandoned by the major industrial countries—this marked the end of the Bretton Woods system.

Bibliography

Barger, Harold. *Outlay and Income in the United States, 1921–1938*. New York: National Bureau of Economic Research, 1942.

Barro, Robert J. "Rational Expectations and the Role of Monetary Policy." *Journal of Monetary Economics* 2 (1976): 1–32.

———. "Unanticipated Money Growth and Unemployment in the United States." *American Economic Review* 67 (1977): 101–15.

———. "Long-Term Contracting, Sticky Prices, and Monetary Policy." *Journal of Monetary Economics* 3 (1977): 305–16.

———. "A Stochastic Equilibrium Model of an Open Economy Under Flexible Exchange Rates." *Quarterly Journal of Economics* 92 (1978): 149–64.

———. "Unanticipated Money, Output, and the Price Level in the United States." *Journal of Political Economy* 86 (1978): 549–80.

———. "The Equilibrium Approach to Business Cycles." Working Paper. Rochester, N.Y.: University of Rochester, November 1979.

Barro, Robert J., and Fischer, Stanley. "Recent Developments in Monetary Theory." *Journal of Monetary Economics* 2 (1976): 133–67.

Barro, Robert J., and Grossman, Herschel I. *Money, Employment and Inflation*. Cambridge, Eng.: Cambridge University Press, 1976.

Barro, Robert J., and Rush, Mark. "Unanticipated Money and Economic Activity." In Stanley Fischer, ed., *Rational Expectations and Economic Policy*. Chicago: University of Chicago Press, 1980, pp. 23–71.

Bernanke, Ben S. "Nonmonetary Effects of the Financial Crisis in the Propagation of the Great Depression." *American Economic Review* 73 (1983): 257–76.

Brunner, Karl, ed. *The Great Depression Revisited*. Boston: Martinus Nijhoff Publishing, 1981.

Brunner, Karl; Cukierman, Alex; and Meltzer, Allan H. "Stagflation, Persistent Unemployment and the Permanence of Economic Shocks." *Journal of Monetary Economics* 6 (1980): 467–92.

Cagan, Phillip. *Determinants and Effects of Changes in the Stock of Money, 1875–1960*. New York: National Bureau of Economic Research, 1965.

Carré, Jean-Jacques; Dubois, Paul; and Malinvaud, Edmond. *La Croissance française: Un Essai d'analyse économique causale de l'après-guerre*. Paris: Seuil, 1972.

Coddington, Alan. "Keynesian Economics: The Search for First Principles." *Journal of Economic Literature* 14 (1976): 1258–273.

Coulbois, Paul. *Finance Internationale*, Vol. 1, *Le Change*. Paris: Cujas, 1979.

Eckstein, Otto. *The Great Recession*. New York: North-Holland, 1978.

Feinstein, C. H. *National Income, Expenditure and Output of the United Kingdom, 1855–1965*. Cambridge, Eng.: Cambridge University Press, 1972.

Fischer, Stanley. "Long-Term Contracts, Rational Expectations and the Optimal Money Supply Rule." *Journal of Political Economy* 85 (1977): 191–205.

Frenkel, Jacob. "Exchange Rates, Prices, and Money: Lessons from the 1920's." *American Economic Review* 70 (1980): 235–42.

Friedman, Milton. "The Role of Monetary Policy." *American Economic Review* 58 (1968): 1–17.

———. "Nobel Lecture: Inflation and Unemployment." *Journal of Political Economy* 85 (1977): 451–72.

Friedman, Milton, and Schwartz, Anna. *A Monetary History of the United States*. New York: National Bureau of Economic Research, 1963.

Gailliot, Henri. "Long Run Determinants of the Distribution of International Monetary Reserves." Ph.D. dissertation, Carnegie-Mellon University, 1973.

Gandolfi, Arthur. "Stability of the Demand for Money During the Great Depression, 1929–1933." *Journal of Political Economy* 82 (1974): 969–83.

Gandolfi, Arthur, and Lothian, James. "Did Monetary Forces Cause the Great Depression?" *Journal of Money, Credit and Banking* 9 (1977): 679–91.

Gordon, Robert J. "Recent Developments in the Theory of Inflation and Unemployment." *Journal of Monetary Economics* 2 (1976): 185–219.

Gordon, Robert J., and Wilcox, James A. "Monetary Interpretations of the Great Depression: An Evaluation and Critique." In Karl Brunner, ed., *The Great Depression Revisited*. Boston: Martinus Nijhoff Publishing, 1981, pp. 49–107.

Haberler, Gottfried. *Prosperity and Depression: A Theoretical Analysis of Cyclical Movements*. 3d ed. Cambridge, Mass.: Harvard University Press, 1960.

———. *The World Economy, Money and the Great Depression, 1919–1939*. Foreign Affairs Studies. Washington, D.C.: American Enterprise Institute, 1976.

Hayek, Friedrich A. von. "The Use of Knowledge in Society." *American Economic Review* 35 (1945): 519–30.

Hicks, John R. *Value and Capital*. 2d ed. Oxford: Oxford University Press, 1946.

Howson, Susan. *Domestic Monetary Management in Britain, 1919–1938*. Cambridge, Eng.: Cambridge University Press, 1975.

IMF. *World Economic Outlook*. Washington, D.C., May 1983.

Jonung, Lars. *The Depression in Sweden and the United States: A Comparison of Causes and Policies*. Lund, Sweden: University of Lund, 1978.

———. "Knut Wicksell's Norm of Price Stabilization and Swedish Monetary Policy in the 1930's." *Journal of Monetary Economics* 5 (1979): 459–96.

Kantor, Brian. "Rational Expectations and Economic Thought." Working Paper. Pittsburgh, Pa.: Carnegie-Mellon University, 1978.

———. "The British Experience in the Interwar Period." Working Paper. Pittsburgh, Pa.: Carnegie-Mellon University, 1979.

Keynes, John Maynard. *The General Theory of Employment, Interest and Money*. London: Macmillan, 1936.

Kindleberger, Charles P. *The World in Depression, 1929–1939*. Berkeley and Los Angeles: University of California Press, 1973.

———. *Manias, Panics and Crashes: A History of Financial Crises*. New York: Basic Books, 1978.

League of Nations. *World Economic Survey*. Geneva, 1932.

———. *Industrialization and Foreign Trade*. Geneva, 1945.

Leijonhufvud, Axel. *Keynes and the Classics*. London: Institute of Economic Affairs, 1969.

———. "Keynes and the Keynesians: A Suggested Interpretation." In Robert W. Clower, ed., *Monetary Theory*. Harmondsworth, Eng.: Penguin, 1969, pp. 298–310.

Lewis, William Arthur. *Economic Survey, 1919–1939*. London: George Allen & Unwin, 1949.

Lucas, Robert E. "Expectations and the Neutrality of Money." *Journal of Economic Theory* 4 (1972): 103–24.

———. "Some International Evidence on Output-Inflation Tradeoffs." *American Economic Review* 63 (1973): 326–34.

———. "An Equilibrium Model of the Business Cycle." *Journal of Political Economy* 83 (1975): 1113–144.

———. "Econometric Policy Evaluation." *Journal of Monetary Economics*, supplement (1976): 19–46.

———. "Understanding Business Cycles." *Journal of Monetary Economics*, supplement (1977): 7–30.

———. "Methods and Problems in Business Cycle Theory." Working Paper. Chicago: University of Chicago, March 1980.

———. "Rules, Discretion, and the Role of the Economic Advisor." In Stanley Fischer, ed., *Rational Expectations and Economic Policy*. Chicago: University of Chicago Press, 1980, pp. 199–210.

Lucas, Robert E., and Rapping, Leonard. "Real Wages, Employment, and Inflation." *Journal of Political Economy* 77 (1969): 721–54.

Mayer, Thomas. "Consumption in the Great Depression." *Journal of Political Economy* 86 (1978): 139–45.

McCallum, Bennett T. "Price Level Adjustments and the Rational Expectations Approach to Macroeconomic Stabilization Policy." *Journal of Money, Credit and Banking* 10 (1978): 418–36.

―――. "Rational Expectations and Macroeconomic Stabilization Policy: An Overview." Working Paper. Charlottesville: University of Virginia, March 1980.

Meltzer, Allan. "Monetary and Other Explanations of the Start of the Great Depression." *Journal of Monetary Economics* 2 (1976): 455–71.

―――. "Anticipated Inflation and Unanticipated Price Change." *Journal of Money, Credit and Banking* 9 (1977): 182–205.

―――. "Comments on 'Monetary Interpretations of the Great Depression.' " In Karl Brunner, ed., *The Great Depression Revisited.* Boston: Martinus Nijhoff Publishing, 1981, pp. 148–64.

Modigliani, Franco. "The Monetarist Controversy or, Should We Forsake Stabilization Policies?" *American Economic Review* 67 (1977): 1–19.

Muth, John. "Rational Expectations and the Theory of Price Movements." *Econometrica* 29 (1961): 315–35.

OECD. *Historical Statistics, 1960–1980.* Paris, 1982.

―――. *National Accounts, 1951–1980.* Vol. 1. Paris, 1982.

―――. *Economic Outlook.* Paris, December 1983.

―――. *National Accounts, 1952–1981.* Vol. 1. Paris, 1983.

Patinkin, Don. *Money, Interest and Prices.* 2d ed. New York: Harper & Row, 1965.

Phelps, Edmund S. "Money Wage Dynamics and Labor Market Equilibrium." *Journal of Political Economy* 76 (1968): 687–711.

Phelps, Edmund S., and Taylor, John B. "Stabilizing Powers of Monetary Policy Under Rational Expectations." *Journal of Political Economy* 85 (1977): 163–89.

Phelps, Edmund S., et al. *Microeconomic Foundations of Employment and Inflation Theory.* New York: Norton, 1970.

Ratner, Sidney. *The Tariff in American History.* New York: Van Nostrand Co., 1972.

Revue d'Economie Politique (REP). Yearly reviews "Banques," in *France Economique,* supplement of *REP* starting in 1922.

Saint-Etienne, Christian. *La France dans la grande crise, 1929–1939: Un Modèle d'équilibre avec anticipations rationnelles.* Ph.D. dissertation, Sorbonne, 1981.

―――. "L'Offre et la demande de monnaie dans la France de l'entre-deux-guerres (1920–1939)." *Revue Economique* 34 (1983): 344–67.

Sargent, Thomas J. "Rational Expectations, the Real Rate of Interest, and the Natural Rate of Unemployment." *Brookings Papers on Economic Activity* 2 (1973): 429–80.

―――. "A Classical Macroeconomic Model for the United States." *Journal of Political Economy* 84 (1976): 207–38.

―――. *Macroeconomic Theory.* New York: Academic Press, 1979.

Sargent, Thomas J., and Wallace, Neil. "Rational Expectations and the Dynamics of Hyperinflation." *International Economic Review* 14 (1973): 328–50.

———. "Rational Expectations, the Optimal Monetary Instrument, and the Optimal Money Supply Rule." *Journal of Political Economy* 83 (1975): 241–54.

———. "Rational Expectations and the Theory of Economic Policy." *Journal of Monetary Economics* 2 (1976): 169–83.

Sauvy, Alfred. *Histoire économique de la France entre les deux guerres*. 4 vols. Paris: Fayard, 1965–1975.

Sayers, Richard S. *The Bank of England, 1891–1944* (vol. 12 and appendixes). Cambridge, Eng.: Cambridge University Press, 1976.

Schwartz, Anna. "Understanding 1929–1933." In Karl Brunner, ed., *The Great Depression Revisited*. Boston: Martinus Nijhoff Publishing, 1981, pp. 5–48.

Shackle, George L. S. *Expectations in Economics*. 2d ed. Cambridge, Eng.: Cambridge University Press, 1952.

Sheppard, David K. *The Growth and Role of U.K. Financial Institutions, 1880–1962*. London: Methuen & Co., 1971.

Shiller, Robert J. "Rational Expectations and the Dynamic Structure of Macroeconomic Models: A Critical Review." *Journal of Monetary Economics* 4 (1978): 1–44.

Steinherr, A. *The Great Depression: A Repeat in the 1980s*. EEC Economic Papers. Brussels, 1982.

Temin, Peter. *Did Monetary Forces Cause the Great Depression?* New York: Norton, 1976.

Tobin, James. "How Dead Is Keynes?" *Economic Inquiry* 15 (1977): 459–68.

———. "Are New Classical Models Plausible Enough to Guide Policy?" *Journal of Money, Credit and Banking* 12 (1980): 788–99.

U.S. Department of Commerce. *Historical Statistics of the United States, Colonial Times to 1970*. Washington, D.C.: Government Printing Office, 1975.

Walters, Alan. "Consistent Expectations, Distributed Lags and the Quantity Theory," *Economic Journal* 81 (1971): 273–81.

Index

Abnormal Importations Act, 28
Agricultural Adjustment Act, 40
Agricultural Marketing Act, 13
Apportionment of Representatives to the U.S. Congress, 10–11
Austria, 16–17
Austro-German protocol, 17
Autonomous spending, 52, 57–59

Banco Ambrosiano, 115
Banking Act of 1933, 36, 40
Banking holiday, 36
Basel Concordat, 114–15
Basel communiqué, 115–16
Blum, Léon, 42
Board of Trade, 28
Britain, *see* United Kingdom
Business cycles (U.S.), 20–21, 29, 33, 55, 67–68

Central Europe: economic problems in 1920s and 1930s, 16–17, 32
Communications Act, 41
Compensation of employees, 66–67
Council for Mutual Economic Assistance (COMECON), 71
Counterpurchase, 93
Countertrade, 93

Creditanstalt, 16–17, 47
Crowding out: in France, 38; in the industrial countries, 88, 91
Current account: British, 22–23; developing countries, 72–75; industrial countries, 72–73

Danat Bank, 17
Davis-Bacon Act, 40
Debt, *see* International debt
Debt rescheduling, 75, 98, 102–3, 116–17
Debt service, 75–76, 107–10
Decision-making under uncertainty, 51–53, 96
Deflation, 7, 25, 35–38, 55–57, 59–60
Demand for money, 51–55
Developing countries, 64; growth outlook, 71; balance of payments and international debt, 72–79
Disinflationary crisis of 1980–1982, 97–98
Dollar, 21, 25, 37, 71–72, 97

Eckstein, Otto, 81
Economic structures, 69–70, 78–79, 88–91, 99–100

European Economic Community (EEC), 63, 64–67
Exchange rate policies, 21–22, 24–26, 37, 103, 123

Farm crisis, *see under* United States
Federal Reserve (U.S.), 20, 21, 24, 32, 35–37, 44–45, 56, 71–72, 98, 103, 123
Fiscal policy: in 1930s, 38–42; in modern period, 88–91
Fishery Cooperative Marketing Act, 41
France: in 1920s, 4, 6–7; in Great Depression, 25, 28–29, 37–41, 57; trade policy, 28–29; monetary policy, 37–38; fiscal policy, 38, 41; in modern period, 65, 90
Free trade, 111–113
Friedman, Milton, 20, 35, 44–45

Germany: in 1920s, 8–9; financial crisis, 16–17; trade policy, 28
Genoa Conference, 21
Gold exchange standard, 21, 43
Gold Reserve Act, 25
Gold standard, 21, 43
Great Depression: in the U.S., 18–21, 24–25, 29, 32–41 *passim*, 44–50, 55–59; in the U.K., 22–24, 28–29; 38–41, 57; in France, 25, 28–29, 37–41, 57; in Germany, 26, 28, 34; causes, 29–33; mechanism, 55–57
Great Recession (U.S.), 79, 81–82
Great Stagnation, 94

Hawley-Smoot Tariff, 13–15, 20, 21, 28–35 *passim*, 46, 47, 55
Hoover, Herbert, 13–14, 17, 20, 32

Industrial countries, 64
Inflation, 67–68, 81, 96, 97

Institutions: national, 100; international, 100–101
Interest rates, 87–88
International banking system, 75–78, 114–18
International debt, 72–78, 100–104, 107–10
International financial system: in 1920s and 1930s, 21–26; in modern period, 72–78, 100–101, 114–18
International lending, 114–118
International Monetary Fund (IMF), 63, 98, 101
International trade: in 1920s and 1930s, 26–29, 30–32; in the modern period, 77–80, 91–93

Japan: in 1920s, 18, 34; in 1970s, 64, 65
Jonung, Lars, 59, 60

Kantor, Brian, 22
Keynesian theories, *see* Autonomous spending, Neo-Keynesian school

Lender of last resort, 114–16
Lucas, Robert E., 52

Macmillan report, 22
Major exporters of manufactures, 64
Maladjustments, 43–44
May report, 22
Meltzer, Allan, 36, 45
Modern structural crisis, 95–97
Monetarist, 52–53
Monetary policy: in 1930s, 34–38; in modern period, 87–88
Money, 51. *See also* Quantity of money, Real money balances
Moratorium, 17
Multifiber Arrangement, 92
Multilateral lending, 116–17

Multilateral trade, 112–13
Muth, John, 52

National Income and Product
  Accounts: U.S., 47; U.K., 48;
  France, 49
Neoclassical school, 51–52
Neo-Keynesian school, 52–53
National Industrial Recovery Act
  (NIRA), 40
National Labor Relations Act, 41
Non-oil developing countries, *see* De-
  veloping countries
Norris–La Guardia Act, 40

Organization for Economic Coopera-
  tion and Development (OECD), 63;
  OECD area, 64–72, 77–79, 88–91
Oil, 68
Oil-exporting countries, *see* Develop-
  ing countries
Ottawa Conference, 28

Panic multiplier, 77
Poincaré, Raymond, 6–7, 37
Popular Front, 25, 42
Pound sterling, 21–24
Price system, 51–53
Productivity, 66
Projections of debt-service burden,
  107–10
Protectionism: in 1930s, 26–29; in
  modern period, 91–93

Quantity of money, 51, 53. *See also*
  Money, Real money balances

Ratner, Sidney, 15
Rational Expectations school, 52
Real money balances, 51–57 *passim.*
  See also Money, Quantity of money

Regulatory practices, 39–41
Reparations, 6, 43
Rescheduling, *see* Debt rescheduling
Roaring Twenties, 4
Robinson-Patman Act, 41
Roosevelt, Franklin D., 25, 36

Schwartz, Anna, 20, 35, 44–45
Securities Act, 40–41
Securities Exchange Act, 41
Social transfers, 88–91
South American debt: in 1930s, xiv–
  xv; in modern period, 75–77
Spending hypothesis, 44–46
Sterling, *see* Pound sterling
Structural crisis, *see* Modern structural
  crisis
Subsidies, *see* Social transfers
Supervision, 114–16
Sweden, 59–60

Temin, Peter, 44
Tokyo Round, 91
Trade, *see* Free trade, International
  trade
Transfers, *see* Social transfers

Uncertainty, 51–53
United Kingdom: in 1920s, 4–6; in
  Great Depression, 21–24, 28–29,
  34–35, 39–40, 58; trade policy, 28–
  29; monetary policy, 34–35; fiscal
  policy, 39–40; in modern period, 65
United States: in 1920s, 4–5, 8–16;
  farm crisis, 8–16; stock exchange,
  20, 36, 44; in Great Depression, 24–
  26, 29, 32–41 *passim*, 44–50, 55–
  59; monetary policy, 35–37, 67–68,
  71; fiscal policy, 38–41, 88–92; in
  modern period, 64–72 *passim*, 79,
  81–83, 88–91, 94–102. *See also*
  Hawley-Smoot Tariff; Federal Reserve

Velocity of money, 51, 55

Wealth effect, 44
World Bank, 117
World Economic and Monetary Con-
    ference, 25, 26